Endors

For the Sake of H.

Praying the Divine Mercy Chaplet with Scripture and Art

For the Sake of His Sorrowful Passion is a lovely book based on the Chaplet of Divine Mercy and is rooted in author Meggie K. Daly's personal conversion story—a story that connects with the reader and the universal need for God's mercy. Many already use her book, *Bead by Bead*, to meditate on the Holy Rosary. Now comes, *For the Sake of His Sorrowful Passion*, incorporating not only the Chaplet of Divine Mercy, but also the Stations of the Cross. Best of all, every scripture passage chosen is heart-felt. A wonderful means of meditation that brings us closer to God. I not only recommend it, I use it!

KAYE PARK HINCKLEY
Award-winning author of nine novels, including *The Wind that Shakes the Corn* and *Absence*, short stories, and blogger

Meggie K. Daly's new book, *For the Sake of His Sorrowful Passion*, is a beautiful meditational book that will help readers to understand and focus more deeply on the passion and death of Christ via the Divine Mercy Chaplet. Her personal story is inspiring, and the information on St. Faustina and the origins of the chaplet are fascinating. The artwork is breathtaking, and the meditations are spot on. Whether you are someone who has regularly prayed the Divine Mercy Chaplet or are new to this devotion, I highly recommend this book!

ELLEN GABLE HRKACH
Author, editor, publisher, past president of the Catholic Writers Guild

There is no other book like *For the Sake of His Sorrowful Passion.* It's a most necessary and useful aid to praying the Divine Mercy Chaplet with multiple options of entering the Passion narrative. Part confession, part history, part prayer book—I loved it all.

VIJAYA BODACH
Author of the novel, *Bound*, Catholic convert, and blogger

For the Sake of His Sorrowful Passion:

Praying the Divine Mercy Chaplet with Scripture and Art

Meggie K. Daly

Cover design: James Hrkach

Cover art: The Divine Mercy Sanctuary, Roman Catholic Basilica, Krakow, Poland. 4-24-14, © Paszkiewicz / Shutterstock.com

Painting of Saint Faustina on pg. v is declared Public domain by the copyright administrator at Marians of the Immaculate Conception, commons.wikimedia.org/wiki/File:200px-Faustina.jpg#filehistory

Misericordia Publishing, United States of America
https://misericordiapublishing.com

ISBN: 978-1-735-2388-0-7 (Full Color Print Edition)
ISBN: 978-1-735-2388-1-4 (Black & White Print Edition)
ISBN: 978-1-735-2388-2-1 (Kindle)
ISBN: 978-1-735-2388-3-8 (EPUB)

DEDICATION

To St. Faustina Kowalska (1905-1938)

In gratitude for the gift of your *Diary*, in acknowledgment of your prayers for sinners like me, and in honor of your heroic example of redemptive suffering.

St. Faustina, pray for us.

Oh, if only the suffering soul knew how it is loved by God, it would die of joy and excess of happiness! Someday, we will know the value of suffering, but then we will no longer be able to suffer. The present moment is ours. (*Diary*, 963)
~ St. Faustina Kowalska

CONTENTS

Throughout the ages, there have been so-called "private" revelations, some of which have been recognized by the authority of the Church. They do not belong, however, to the deposit of faith. It is not their role to improve or complete Christ's definitive Revelation, but to help live more fully by it in a certain period of history. Guided by the Magisterium of the Church, the sensus fidelium knows how to discern and welcome in these revelations whatever constitutes an authentic call of Christ or his saints to the Church. (para 67, CCC)

ACKNOWLEDGMENTS

Excerpts from the book, *Divine Mercy in My Soul, (3rd edition),* Saint Maria Faustina Kowalska, (Stockbridge, MA: Marian Press), 2011, are used with permission of the Marian Fathers of the Immaculate Conception of the B.V.M.

When the word, *Diary*, is used in this book, it always refers to *Divine Mercy in My Soul* by Saint Maria Faustina Kowalska, as noted above.

Original Polish *Diary* copyright © 1981
Congregation of Sisters of Our Lady of Mercy Original Polish
Nihil Obstat: Krakow, April 17, 1979, Rev. Ignatius Rozycki
Imprimatur: Krakow, April 18, 1979, Francis Macharski, Abp.

English Translation *Diary* copyright © 1987
Nihil Obstat: George H. Pearce, S.M., Former Abp. of Suva, Fiji
Imprimatur: Joseph F. Maguire, Bp. of Springfield, MA
March 16, 1987

Direct excerpts from the *Diary* are italicized and denote the paragraph number where the quote is found. The words of Jesus cited from the *Diary* are additionally in boldface.

The artwork marked as {PD-old-100} is in the Public Doman because its copyright has expired in the United States and countries with a copyright term of no more than the life of the author plus 100 years. This copyright expiration includes all countries where this book is distributed. The author's access was through Wikipedia Commons.

All artwork is used with permission or is in the Public Domain due to copyright expiration.

The names used in "Part 1 - Personal" of this book, including my own, are pseudonyms to respect the privacy of all.

IN GRATITUDE

Shortly after publishing my first book, *Bead by Bead: The Scriptural Rosary*, on the centennial anniversary of the Feast of Our Lady of Fatima, I knew that I wanted to create a similar resource for the Divine Mercy Chaplet. Slowly, the organization of this book became apparent to me. Additional clarification came while teaching a class on Divine Mercy at my local parish.

I want to thank the participants in that class for their contribution, encouragement, and giving me the chance to share my love for everything Divine Mercy: Connie, Dene, Jackie, Jane, Jeanne, Karen, Katie, Larry, Lothar, Nick, Sarah, Shirley, and Tina.

For that class, I drew on heavily on various books: The *Diary* of St. Faustina, *The Second Greatest Story Ever Told* by Fr. Michael Gaitley, MIC, and two books about St Faustina—one by Maria Tarnawaska written before St. Faustina's canonization and the other by Ewa K. Czaczkowska written five years after her canonization. I also used the first-half of the FORMED series Divine Mercy by Fr. Michael Gaitley, M.I.C.

Thanks to my beta readers: Bart Gallant, Cindy Olson, Larry Rosemeyer, and Linda Watson, for your encouragement and input, which improved the manuscript. Especial thanks go to Kaye Hinckley and Vijaya Bodach, your critiques were excellent and insightful. Thank you, one and all for the gracious gift of your time!

Editors are the unsung heroes of book polishing and publishing. Kudos to my editor, Ellen Gable Hrkach. Your attention to detail is phenomenal, and your prompting for more detail on my conversion experience was sagacious.

Thanks to James Hrkach for his winning artistic interpretation of my crude book cover design. As always, he turns my mediocre designs into exceptional art.

Prayers, charity, and friendships do make a difference. Many thanks to those who have been and are still part of my story.

Thanks to the Marian Fathers of the Immaculate Conception of the B.V.M. for spreading the message of Divine Mercy throughout the world. And special recognition, to Fr. Michael E. Gaitley, M.I.C., who has touched so many lives through the fire of his faith and love for Divine Mercy.

Praise and thanksgiving to Jesus Christ for providing the great blessings of the Divine Mercy devotions through His servant, St. Faustina. Thanks to Our Blessed Mother for her gift of the Rosary.

CHAPTER 1

INTRODUCTION

I started reading the *Diary* of St. Faustina before the delivery driver returned to the bottom of the long, winding driveway that connected our fourteen acres into County Home Road. After liberating the *Diary* from its corrugated brown wrapper, I wrote "April 17, 2012" just inside the burgundy leather cover, as if the date was important to document.

I wish that this book, *For the Sake of His Sorrowful Passion*, had been written—by someone else, of course—and that I'd read it first to illuminate my literary and spiritual journey through the *Diary*.

Nevertheless, I was captivated by the *Diary*, and upon completion of its 692 pages several weeks later, I began praying the Divine Mercy Chaplet daily. I've never stopped. The message of Divine Mercy grabbed my heart then as it does today.

Some eight years later, 2020 is a year many would like to forget, myself included. Still, positive side effects of the coronavirus pandemic, a diagnosis of breast cancer, and four surgeries in four months were unforeseen pockets of time and a laser focus on my mortality to bring this long-overdue project to completion.

The remaining eight chapters of this book fall naturally into three parts: Personal, Historical, and Prayerful.

Part One – Personal begins in Chapter 2 with the story of how I experienced the blessings of the Divine Mercy Chaplet before I knew anything of St. Faustina, her *Diary*, or the Divine Mercy Chaplet. I believe that the Chaplet of Divine Mercy, prayed on my behalf (and unknown to me at the time), brought me back to Holy Mother Church.

Jesus encouraged St. Faustina to pray the Divine Mercy Chaplet nonstop and to meditate on His passion and death as she prayed. Chapter 3 explores why the Paschal Sacrifice is so pleasing to God the Father, and the tight coupling of Divine Mercy to the passion and death of the Son.

Part Two – Historical starts with my attempt to know, as I would a good friend, the woman whose *Diary* so impacted me. Who was this Helena Kowalska? Yes, she was born in 1905, died at the age of thirty-three, and canonized as St. Faustina in 2000—but those demographic details tell us nothing of the child, the teenager, the young woman, or the saint herself who inadvertently left us an astonishing and strange *Diary*. I was mesmerized by this woman's intimacy with Jesus, as reflected in her *Diary*. I hungered to know everything about Helena's life.

The *Diary* of St. Maria Faustina of the Blessed Sacrament is not an easy read. Sometimes events that occurred in the past are mixed in with current happenings with the salient dates unspecified. Any diary or journal is a personal reflection, as it was for St. Faustina. She wrote it to chronicle her inner life for her confessor and spiritual advisor, Fr. Michael Sopocko, S.J. He didn't have adequate time to spend with this unusual religious sister in the confessional. He needed more information and time to digest what she was telling him.

Like the writings of all canonized Saints, Sr. Faustina's *Diary* is not part of the Deposit of Faith and falls into the category of "private" revelation. Such writings are a useful lens on the saints' intimacy with God filtered through their unique personality and life experiences.

Theologians of the Holy See scrutinized her *Diary*, most notably by Very Rev. Fr. Ignatius Rozycki, an early critic. He became a crucial promoter of the *Diary*. The Church has declared with ecclesiastical authority that there is nothing contrary to our Catholic faith in the *Diary*. Based on her *Diary* and the testimony of others regarding her virtuous life, St. Faustina has been recommended for consideration as a doctor of the Church.[1]

Two books provided an invaluable background for St. Faustina's biography in Chapter 4. The first book was published before her canonization, *Sister Faustina Her Life and Mission* by Maria Tarnawaska.[2] The second book was released shortly after her canonization, *Faustina: The Mystic & Her Message* by Ewa K. Czaczkowska.[3]

Although I don't go into detail in this short book, St. Faustina was devoted to the Mother of God. *The Purest of Lilies* by Fr. Donald Calloway, MIC., is a detailed study of the impact of the Blessed Mother on her spirituality and highlights the St. Faustina's mystical experiences with Mary.[4]

The Divine Mercy Chaplet is one of five Divine Mercy devotions we find in the *Diary*, and it is the primary focus of the meditations in Part Three of this book. However, it is essential to understand all five—they are interconnected. Chapter 5 contains background information on all five devotions and describes the promises associated with each, based on Jesus's words as recorded in the *Diary*.

Part Three – Prayerful is a resource for meditations while praying the Divine Mercy Chaplet. I wanted to create a meditation guide similar to what I had created for the Rosary in my book, *Bead by Bead: The Scriptural Rosary*.[5]

A young seminarian once told me it only took him seven minutes to pray the Divine Mercy Chaplet—it takes me longer than that. I use the visualization techniques of St. Ignatius of Loyola to place myself alongside Christ during His passion and death. I believe that I can be "present" with Christ in a unique way due to His Incarnation.

Through the Incarnation, Jesus Christ is fully man and fully God. His human nature allowed Him to participate in time as we experience it—linearly with a past, present, and future. His divine nature includes full participation in the Godhead of the Trinity and allowed Him to exist outside of time, in an ever-present eternity without beginning and end. Our human mind can't understand eternity or the Incarnation any more than an ant can understand the theory of relativity. Yet we believe this to be true if we are Christians.

Thus, temporal events that Christ has participated in are "God-events" that took place in history, yet remain ever-present outside of time in eternity.[6] Hence we can unite ourselves with the passion of Christ in a mystical way that transcends time. In a related way, the priest re-presents the Paschal Sacrifice during Mass without a re-crucifixion of Christ.

Chapter 6 is a short tutorial on how to pray the Divine Mercy Chaplet for those new to this devotion. It includes the words for required and optional prayers as well as a diagram.

Chapter 7 partitions fifteen distinct events from the passion and death of Christ, for which we have detailed written accounts in Scripture, and breaks them in three chronological Sequences: I, II, III. Each Sequence contains five decades, and each decade contains ten Scriptures coupled with a fine-art image for each decade, thus corresponding to one complete Divine Mercy Chaplet.

Chapters 8 maps the Stations of the Cross into three Sequences: I, II, III, each with five decades. Each decade has an image paired with the Station of the Cross and short mediations that I have composed. My meditations are suggestive, not prescriptive. Over time you will create your own "songs" of glory, praise, thanksgiving, and petition.

I often combine my Rosary with my Divine Mercy Chaplet on the days that I meditate on the Sorrowful Mysteries. Chapter 9 explains how I integrate my Divine Mercy Chaplet into my Rosary, through the hands of the Blessed Virgin Mary. I share what works for me; perhaps it can work for you, too.

PART ONE – PERSONAL

If the angels were capable of envy, they would envy us for two things: one is the receiving of Holy Communion, and the other is suffering. (Diary, 1804)

CHAPTER 2

DIVINE MERCY AND ME

I pulled my car up to the parish office and turned off the ignition. The date was April 11, 2012, the Wednesday immediately following Easter Sunday. Perhaps my meeting with Fr. Tony, the pastor at the local Catholic Church, would squelch the nebulous internal nagging that I blamed for being here.

The appointment was simple enough to schedule; I called one day and got in the next. That was one benefit of living in a small, sleepy Southern town. Maybe the only one. It had been harder than I anticipated to adjust to leaving San Diego behind; a bit like moving from heaven to purgatory—an analogy, testifying to my Catholic upbringing.

Like most driven personality types, I preferred to be in control. I didn't schedule meetings without knowing the purpose, and with someone that I didn't know, especially a Catholic priest. Ambiguity wasn't welcome in my comfort zone.

What did it matter if Fr. Tony thought I was crazy? I wasn't a member of his tiny parish; moreover, I hadn't attended Mass for almost twenty years, and back then, it was primarily a cultural habit, not an act of worship.

When Neal and I married on the beach in 2005, we were both non-denominational Christians. Neal wouldn't have married a practicing Catholic, and that, I was not.

I didn't want to be early, so I sat in the car for a few minutes with the air-conditioning running. The building that housed the parish office reminded me of a tired, double-wide trailer, a temporary structure that, over time, acquired permanence and some equally unattractive additions.

The parish secretary greeted me warmly as I entered the cramped reception area. The only available chair, which barely fit next to the door, shared premium space with a printer and a couple of file cabinets to my right. I sat two feet from the front of her desk and listened while she phoned Fr. Tony to let him know of my arrival.

What was I going to say to this priest? What was my game plan? My heart hammered my chest. I started to sweat. *Was it hot and stuffy in there, or was I merely nervous?*

Within minutes a smiling, portly priest with dark hair and an olive-toned complexion squeezed into the reception area through the door that I had just entered. He introduced himself with a friendly handshake and immediately ushered me into a room adjacent to the reception area and twice its size.

He closed the door behind us and plopped into the chair behind the large desk that occupied the middle of the room.

My eyes gravitated to the old-time wood paneling that covered the walls in their entirety. With any luck, the panels had long ago leached their formaldehyde-nastiness into the air. The room lacked any window or natural light; fresh air wasn't an option.

"My office is just a closet—literally. The Director of Religious Education is out today, so we're meeting in her office."

Fr. Tony pointed to the only other chair in the room pushed up against the wall. "Pull up a chair, so we don't have to shout at each other."

I pulled the chair up next to the desk on the side opposite to Fr. Tony and positioned it halfway between where he sat and the door, not too close but not too far away from where Fr. Tony sat.

"What can I do for you, Ms. Daly?" Fr. Tony's doe-like, brown eyes smiled expectantly.

"Please called me Meggie."

"Excellent. What can I do for you, *Meggie*?"

"Um, I'd like to say a prayer before we start, Father. Okay?"

"Sure, go right ahead." He smiled broadly. I needed some guidance. Badly.

Without making the Sign of the Cross, I bowed my head, closed my eyes, and waited for the words to come. My prayer went something like this:

"Dear Father, I am here today meeting with Fr. Tony because I believe that you called me here. Holy Spirit, guide this conversation to where you want it to go. I ask this in the name of Your Son, Jesus. Amen."

Fr. Tony echoed my Amen.

When I looked up, Father was smiling with his hand clasped in front of him on the desk. It reminded me of how the Sisters of St. Joseph of Carondelet had taught us to sit in our wooden "sleigh" desks with our hands folded in front of us.

"Okay. Now how can I help you, Meggie?"

"I'm not sure, Father. I just felt like I was supposed to meet with you. That probably sounds weird, doesn't it?"

I didn't share the annoying pronouncement that my eldest son, Sean, had made last Thanksgiving. "Get serious, Mom. Do your homework. If you're going to be a Christian, you've got to be Catholic."

I prayed daily for Sean to receive the gift of Christian faith, but his academically-motivated declaration kept working its way into my psyche. Sean and I were an awful lot alike, especially at his age, when I thought I knew it all.

"Well, why don't you tell me about yourself?" Fr. Tony suggested.

Perfect, I can do that. I explained why Neal and I had relocated to this small rural community, the makeup of our blended family, when we got married, what we did for a living—cocktail party talk—the kind of things that cost nothing to share.

He shared a bit about himself. He had grown up in Philadelphia, his previous diocesan and pastoral assignments before landing his current position—which he loved because everything was slow and easy, the very things that grated on me.

The priest was gentle, warm, and jolly—like an Italian Santa Claus. He put me completely at ease.

Without a conscious decision to spill my guts, a calm settled over me, accompanied by a pressing desire to share my story with him.

First, I warned him, "This will be the most shocking, horrible story you probably have ever heard."

He said, "I doubt that is the case. I've been a priest for a long time." *Was he chuckling?* It didn't matter, everything about Fr. Tony, his face, his body language, his voice, communicated, "Be at Peace,

Meggie, I'm on your side."

I waded into vulnerable territory—adoptive parents, problems bonding, multiple marriages, finding birth parents, annulments, counseling, and mortal sins that would be hard to share even within the secrecy of a confessional. I morphed into a raw, blubbering, red-faced mess.

Fr. Tony kept the supply of tissues coming my way and asked a few questions here and there, perhaps to reassure me that he was carefully listening, but mostly he let me talk. Without sparing any details, I shared my pre-conversion life of shame with no excuses, my conversion experience, and my post-conversion life as a non-denominational Protestant.

The time passed quickly but long enough for me to soak the front of my shirt with tears and create a mountain of snotty tissues in my lap. I asked Father what I had always wanted to ask a Catholic priest about my conversion experience.

In my late forties, while successful professionally, I was depressed over the mess of my personal life and saw no way to "fix" things. I'd no sense of God in my life and certainly didn't believe that Jesus was God. In the proceeding sixteen months, I'd been hospitalized twice for what initially appeared to be heart attacks. The second episode landed me in ICU and nearly claimed my life. None of this drew me to spiritual reformation but oddly seemed to push me further away from God. I sunk deeper into despair.

In January of 2004, less than four months after my discharge from ICU, I had a vision that changed my life forever. At the time, I was confident that I was fully awake—but maybe it was a dream...

My bedroom glowed with a brilliant soft light, emanating from a man who hovered above me and to my right. I sat up in bed to make sure I was awake. Everything about his appearance was dazzling, his face, his white flowing garments, his shoulder-length dark hair. He extended both arms out to me, silently and invitingly; His wordless message was, "Come to me."

I did not doubt that this person was Jesus Christ. Although I was in a state of mortal sin, there was no condemnation in his gaze. That night, I experienced complete love, acceptance, and forgiveness; an overpowering peace engulfed me.

Whether a dream or not matters little; what does matter is that I was infused with the knowledge that I'm deeply loved and that nothing I'd done or might do could mar the purity and intensity of that love. In the morning, I fell to my knees and thanked God for the gift of faith. The night ended a lifetime of frightening dreams and the beginning of my journey back into the arms of Jesus Christ, my Lord, and Savior. I've never been the same, praise be to God!

"What do you think I saw, Fr. Tony? What happened to me?" Although it had been over nine years since my life had changed one-hundred and eighty degrees, the event that changed my life was still fresh in my mind.

"I think you experienced the Divine Mercy of God," Fr. Tony replied without any hesitation. "Would you like absolution for your sins?"

"Did I just go to Confession?

"Yes, you did. You confessed your sins, expressed sorrow for your sins, and tried to make amends to those hurt by your sins."

Without analyzing if I had satisfied the five criteria for a good Confession, I resounded with a tearful but joyful, "Yes!" At that moment, all I cared about was drinking the cup of mercy that Fr. Tony was offering through Mother Church.

He held up his hand towards me in the gesture of absolution, closed his eyes, and prayed, "God the Father of mercies, through the death and resurrection of his Son, has reconciled the world to himself and sent the Holy Spirit among us for the forgiveness of sins; through the ministry of the Church, may God give you pardon and peace, and I absolve you from your sins in the name of the Father, and of the Son, and of the Holy Spirit. Amen."

My heart danced as Fr. Tony prayed the healing words that I hadn't heard for decades.

"I hate to disappoint you, but that is not the worst Confession that I have ever heard in my life," Fr. Tony said, with a twinkle in his eyes.

"Really?" I was incredulous.

"Nope. Not even close." He crossed his arms in front of him and sat back, sporting a big smile.

At that point, he asked me if I would like to make my way back into the full graces of the Catholic Church.

"Yes!" I replied without a moment's thought.

Fr. Tony volunteered to be my advocate through the annulment process and asked me to schedule a separate meeting to discuss the details.[1] He was optimistic that the Church would have sufficient grounds to grant a decree of nullity on my prior marriage—the one before Neal.

Neal would have to go through a separate annulment process for his previous marriage if he was willing. I would need a positive outcome for both Neal and my annulments for our marriage to be recognized by the Catholic Church.

Fr. Tony knew his "stuff." I found out during that part of our conversation that he had a Licentiate of Canon Law degree. Neal's prior marriage lacked proper form since he'd married a baptized (though not practicing) Catholic outside the Church.

I thanked Fr. Tony profusely for his time. He asked me to contact the receptionist to set up our next meeting. I would do that after I spoke to Neal. I had no idea how Neal would react to my decision to return to the Catholic Church—and I wasn't sure what that might mean for Neal and me as a couple.

Driving home, I reflected on the blessing of meeting with Fr. Tony, how generous he'd been with his time and his gentle, non-judgmental spirit. Connecting with this priest—a canon lawyer assigned to a tiny Catholic parish of fewer than 150 families—was no coincidence.

I doubted that this turn of events would have transpired in San Diego. Neal and I had been comfortable in our worship community there. The benefits of living in this rural community, that I was struggling to call home, hit me on the head like a hammer. It had to be God's plan!

I couldn't wait to share my excitement with Blanche, my best friend from college. My brain was already constructing an email to send her the minute that I got home.

Blanche and I had remained close friends through most of our twenties. But the messier my life became, the less my life matched Blanche's squeaky-clean Catholic life as wife and mother. Life was busy for both of us. I wasn't motivated to maintain a long-distance friendship with Blanche, who would've disapproved of my choices anyway.

Shortly after Neal and I moved to his southern hometown, I'd wondered about Blanche. A simple query located Blanche and her husband's business on the internet. On a whim, I sent a contact email to the company, which eventually found its way to Blanche. We rekindled our friendship about nine months before I met with Fr.

Tony.

Blanche was ecstatic that I had developed a strong Christian faith, yet she struggled to understand how I could leave the Catholic Church, her most cherished gift.

Leaving was easy to explain. I was happy with Neal, our Protestant faith, and to be free from what I perceived as the rigidity of Catholicism. Besides, there was no way back to the Catholic Church—I'd been married too many times. But that was before Fr. Tony ladled on his kindness, granted me absolution, and infused me with hope for a reconciliation. It was also before subsequent research enlightened me to what the Catholic Church actually taught as opposed to what I thought.

Several weeks before Easter 2012, Blanche and I had exchanged a flurry of emails. I was struggling to find a faith community to worship with in my new town. Via email, I'd told Blanche that I was going to meet with the pastor at the little Catholic church that served the whole county without explaining why—I couldn't anyway. She told me that she would be praying for me.

I sent Blanche the following email the afternoon after meeting with Fr. Tony:

From: Meggie
Sent: Wednesday, April 11, 2012 3:36 PM
To: Blanche
Subject: Meeting today

Dear Blanche –

Thank you for your prayers. I have been trying to be very open to the work of the Holy Spirit in my life. I spoke with the local priest, Fr. Tony, about my previous marriage and a possible annulment. I also shared with Fr. Tony, my personal testimony about how I came to know and love the Lord. He helped me understand the miracle of my conversion more fully. He and I relate well. He is willing to be my advocate should I decide to proceed on a petition for annulment.

Many things trouble me about the [Catholic] *Church's teachings—but I have books to study from Fr. Tony. He is willing to invest time in my search for truth and my Church community. Father is about our age. He is wise in the ways of family dynamics, etc. I am on a journey home. I will stop at nothing to be united as closely as I can to my dear Lord on this earth.*

If that means the Catholic Church, then I have faith the Lord will lead me there. He has been so faithful and merciful to me.

Love, Meggie

I knew that it would be a while before I heard back from Blanche, she was less enamored with "technology," as she called email, than I was.

My thoughts turned to Neal as I heard his truck coming up the gravel driveway, and much earlier than usual. *How would Neal react to the news that I decided to attend the local Catholic Church?* Neither of us had found any Protestant Churches to our liking. My back and forth self-talk ended once my husband walked in the back door.

"Hey, you're home early. Short day?" I inquired.

"I wanted to work in the barn before dinner. How'd the meeting go with the priest?"

Neal knew that I had made an appointment to see Fr. Tony, without having full-clarity as to why.

"Well...it was amazing!"

"Do tell?"

"You sure? You might not make it out to the barn."

"I'm all ears." Neal sat down at the kitchen table.

"I spent over an hour with Fr. Tony. I ended up telling him my life story. I even told him about my conversion experience; everything just came rolling out nonstop. He's a great listener."

"You told him...everything?" Neal wanted the gory details.

I recounted my meeting. "Fr. Tony said that it sounded like I had a lot of pain in my life. He didn't once judge me. Then he asked me if I would like absolution of my sins!"

"How do you feel about going back to the Catholic Church and receiving absolution from a priest?"

"I feel happier than I have for a long time. Like a huge boulder has been rolled off my shoulders. I made an appointment for a detailed Confession a couple of weeks from now, too."

"Then, I am happy for you."

"Really?"

"Yes, I am."

"I am going to start going to Mass at Immaculate Conception this Sunday. I don't expect you to go with me or anything like that. I just hope you aren't too upset with me. I had no idea that this was going to happen."

Neal walked around to where I stood and gave me a big hug. *There was no rain on this parade so far.*

"Fr. Tony offered to advocate for us to get our marriage recognized by the Catholic Church. A marriage tribunal would have to decide that my marriage to Joe wasn't valid from the Church's perspective from the very beginning. It also means that your marriage to Jules would have to go through the same process.

"Father expects that your petition would be straightforward. A declaration of nullity would be way more complicated for my marriage to Joe, but Fr. Tony thinks it has a good chance, given the details that I shared with him. Can you believe that Fr. Tony is a canon lawyer? He knows the marriage tribunal process inside and out."

"If it's important to you, then, of course, I'll cooperate."

"It is a big deal for me, Neal. There are no guarantees that the tribunal in the diocese, where Joe and I were married, will reach the verdict that I want—and that is scary. But thank you so much for being on board."

Neal's reaction was more positive than I'd dared to imagine.

I called the parish office the next day to make two appointments: one for me to meet with Fr. Tony regarding my annulment and a second, one week later, to hear my "Life Confession." Various resources on the "Examination of Conscience" helped me to prepare for that exhaustive Confession. I kept a-very-patient Fr. Tony in the confessional for forty-five minutes, confessing every sin from my earliest childhood remembrances up to the present. I spent days preparing my itemized list. *God bless Fr. Tony!*

On Friday afternoon, *April 13, 2012,* I made my way from the parking lot up to the little red-brick church across from the rectory where Fr. Tony lived.

The double glass doors to the church were unlocked. I walked past four stained-glass windows, impressive for a little country church, featuring New Testament scenes: The Visitation, Flight into Egypt, Finding Jesus in the Temple, and Miracle of Turning Water into Wine. The corridor in the narthex widened, revealing a stunning, stained-glass window of the Virgin Mary that occupied an entire wall. Streams of sunlight fired pieces of glass into a dizzying array of shades of blue.

Pausing in front of the life-size image of Mary, I inhaled its beauty. I'd missed Mary during my Protestant years—she had been minimized to more or less a random woman, conceived with original sin, who gave birth to Jesus and then other children with Joseph. It had seemed almost disrespectful to me, but the concept of veneration and praying to the saints for intercession was either unknown or denied. When I had the unquestioning faith of an innocent child, I'd felt closer to Mary than anyone else. She was my safe haven; I wanted her back.

The lights were off as I entered the nave of the church. The fragrance of flowers and the seemingly unlikely scent of incense swirled around me. An array of stained-glass windows ran from the back of the church up to the sanctuary. Their multi-colored filtered light guided me to a front pew.

No one else was in the church. The red altar light flickered to the left of the tabernacle, denoting the presence of Christ in the form of the consecrated host.

"Help me to believe, Lord, that You are truly present," I prayed aloud. The Real Presence of Christ in the Eucharist wasn't something I had to wrestle with as a Protestant. It could take years before I would be able to receive the Eucharist, if ever. Annulments are complicated processes with no guarantees, but if that should happen, I wanted to be a committed believer in the Real Presence.

Could there be a path back to the Catholic Church for me? I'd never even considered the Catholic Church as a potential home when I had my conversion experience.

This coming Sunday would be my first Mass in almost two decades. I picked up the paper missalette containing the readings for the Mass and flipped to the readings for the first Sunday after Easter. The heading for this coming Sunday, April 15, read "Divine Mercy Sunday."

How appropriate, I thought, *Divine Mercy Sunday will be my first Mass back in the Catholic Church after many years.* I had certainly experienced God's mercy. He had saved me from both a physical and spiritual death and infused me with the gift of faith overnight. When I last attended a Catholic Mass, there was no feast called Divine Mercy, and the missalette gave no background on Divine Mercy Sunday.

A large image of Christ hung to the right of the altar. The artist portrayed Jesus in a brilliant white robe with his left hand raised, pointing to His heart. His right hand lifted as in a blessing. Two rays, one white and one red, emanated from His heart. His left foot extended out as if walking towards the viewer. The words "Jesus, I trust in You" were at the bottom of the image. Although I'd never seen that painting before, elements of that image were familiar to me.

I hadn't heard back from Blanche, but that evening I sent her another email update.

From: Meggie
To: Blanche
Sent: Friday, April 13, 2012 7:30 PM
Subject: RE: Meeting today

Blanche, my dear sister in Christ –

How precious a gift you are to me! Your encouragement and prayers give me someone to celebrate with—each step that I take. Yes, Neal has endorsed this next phase of my faith journey. Praise be to our God! It will likely take several years to hear back one way or another. But I can wait knowing that God is still working on me. I do believe that the Church is empowered with wisdom to enact His will with respect to my status in the Roman Catholic Church. So whichever way it turns out, I will still have my Lord with me.

This Sat night is my first Mass in almost 20 years—but absolutely the first Mass where I can both rest in the peace in the Lord and possess absolute faith in Him. Fr. Tony told me that my vision in Jan 2004 was experiencing the Divine Mercy of God. It is the only thing that makes sense of what happened and the change it has wrought in my life. The memory of that sweet peace and enveloping love remains the most powerful experience of my life. Do you know that this Sunday's Mass is called the Divine Mercy Sunday? I find this non-coincidental!

Today I just went and sat in the church and drank in the aromas of flowers and incense.

I have learned or remembered so many things incorrectly. Between reading the two books, Catholicism for DUMMIES and The United States Catholic Catechism for Adults—it is awfully difficult to get my other work done.

Pray that God will give me faith in the Eucharist. It is only just that I should not be able to receive communion until I have faith in the Lord's real presence. Being barred from communion, until (and if ever) I am ever a fully practicing Catholic is just another sign of God's caring concern.

What a mysterious God we worship!
Love, Meggie

I heard back from an ecstatic Blanche the very next day. I have reprinted the portion of her email that relates to my journey home.

From: Blanche
To: Meggie
Sent: Saturday, April 14, 2012 3:10 PM
Subject: RE: Meeting today

Dear Meggie,

Your email made my hair stand on end—and that is no coincidence either! Of course, I know this is Divine Mercy Sunday. It is one of my favorite devotions. Are you familiar with it? ***I have been saying a novena for you these last nine days, as Christ requested through St. Faustina.*** [Blanche's emphasis] *The last Pope, John Paul II, who we considered our parish priest while we lived in Rome, died on the eve of Divine Mercy Sunday, and I have just finished reading a biography of his. I actually read about his death on April 2, which was the date of his death a few years ago...*
What a wonderful day to return to Mass! I shall be praying for you tomorrow when I celebrate Divine Mercy...

Love and prayers to you, dear Meggie!
Blanche

I responded to Blanche that evening after doing some internet-based research on St. Faustina, Divine Mercy Sunday, and John Paul II.:

From: Meggie
To: Blanche
Sent: Saturday, April 14, 2012 6:57 PM
Subject: RE: Meeting today

Dear Blanche – Thank you so much for your prayers. I knew nothing of St Faustina—but I have now read about her. I have ordered St. Faustina's Diary. The only reason that I knew about Divine Mercy Sunday was that I stopped into the local Church on Friday to see what the bible readings would be for this Sunday. I knew nothing about the history of Divine Mercy Sunday—nor the image—until I read your email this evening and began researching on the web.

Now that I think back on my meeting with Fr. Tony and describing to him what I saw and his response, I am convinced that he nailed it. His credentials are perhaps a further demonstration of God's divine mercy: Canon Lawyer and Former Judicial Vicar. Perhaps at 3 pm each day, I could ask for your prayer for my full communion with our Lord.

Your sister in Christ, Meggie

In August 2012, Neal's previous marriage to Jules was granted a decree of nullity and received a "Declaration of Freedom," which allowed him to marry in the Catholic Church. That very same month, my husband began the Rite of Christian Initiation Program for Adults with Fr. Tony, entirely on his own volition. Although Neal, a seminary-trained ex-Protestant pastor, completed the RCIA program, he wasn't able to enter the Catholic Church on Holy Saturday 2013—my petition for an ecclesiastical annulment was still in process.

In July 2013, I received a letter that the diocesan tribunal, where I had previously married Joe, had issued an affirmative decision regarding my petition for a declaration of nullity.

In September 2013, I received another notification that the Second Instance Court had upheld the decision of the first court. On October 4, 2013, Neal and my marriage received a radical sanation (*sanatio in radice,* which means "healing in the root"):

> *"This convalidation occurs at the moment the favor is granted; it is retroactive to the moment the marriage was celebrated. It is hereby noted that the present marriage is rendered valid, lawful and indissoluble by Divine law."*

October 5, 2013, the Feast of St. Faustina was a gorgeous Saturday morning. The sun was shining, the birds were singing, and there was no unbearable humidity to taint a perfect day. At the eight a.m. Mass, Neal was received into the Catholic Church by Fr. Tony, through a special arrangement with the Bishop. Neal received his First Holy Communion and Confirmation. We renewed our wedding vows to celebrate the day.

Neal and I were both able to receive the Eucharist on October 5 together as a couple. It was the first time in many, many years that I had received Holy Communion with a clear conscience resting in the peace that Holy Mother Church confers on her prodigal children and with the belief in the True Presence.

We know that all things work together for good for those who love God, who are called according to his purpose. (Rom, 8:28, NRSV)

***

I wasn't prepared for the call that evening several years ago. My biological father, Mel, had been in the hospital since Sunday night and had, without any warning, lost consciousness earlier in the day. He was now on life-support, and his prospects for recovery were poor.

Mel had turned 87 the previous month and seemed in reasonably good health. He'd fought off various health challenges and had won or at least had found a way to manage them with a good quality of life.

Occasionally I'd had nightmares about my late-found father dying, but not because I'd sewn him into the frayed fabric of my life and that of my children. It was his spiritual belief system that troubled me.

His was the widespread spirituality where everyone goes to heaven, and there is no such thing as hell or the devil. And equally seductive, this philosophy requires little self-sacrifice. In other words, "love doesn't hurt."

In my last visit with him the year before he died, I'd asked Mel if he self-identified as Christian; he replied affirmatively. I pointed out that his core "Christian" beliefs didn't jive with the Bible and weren't ones that Jesus would recognize. I reminded him that Jesus frequently spoke about hell and the devil.

I continued praying for him. I know firsthand what it is like to have a stubborn will and closed heart when we are not ready to give up behaviors that a coherent Christian faith requires. I, also, know firsthand that a slight crack allows the mercy of God to regenerate proud and calloused hearts.

Less than two days later, my middle daughter, Bernadette, flew to be with her unconscious grandfather on life-support. When Bernadette arrived, she joined my father's wife and his step-daughter at the hospital. A short time later, two other adult grandchildren joined the family members keeping vigil at his hospital bedside.

As a favor to me, Bernadette asked the little group of family members keeping vigil if they would object to my praying the Divine Mercy Chaplet on speakerphone with Bernadette over her grandfather. She wondered because, to our knowledge, no one in the room would self-identify as a Christian or grew up in a religious household.

No one objected, and it seemed to be a relief. My daughter called me on her cell phone and asked me if I would first like to speak privately to Mel. She put her cell phone up to his ear. I told him goodbye and that I loved him and that we were going to pray for him.

Experts say that hearing is the last sense to fail those who appear to be unconscious or comatose. Bernadette told me later that the only time she saw any movement or response of any type from my father was an eye blink while I was speaking to him.

Now on speakerphone, I explained the logistics of the prayer that I was going to lead. Everyone joined hands, and together as a group, we prayed the Divine Mercy Chaplet. Their response being, "Have mercy on us and on the whole world."

Perhaps some present were praying for a miracle of physical healing. I was praying for protection for my father's soul and that when he came face to face with Jesus, he would cast himself into the incomprehensible mercy of God.

Bernadette stayed with him in his room until he died a few days after they had taken him off life-support. He never did regain consciousness.

St. Faustina writes of being transported to the bed of a dying individual. She could see into the spiritual realm in a way that only a few saints have been able. St. Faustina writes of a terrible battle taking place for the soul of the nearly deceased.[2] She also wrote that Jesus came to one despairing soul (when that person appeared to be dead) three times to offer His mercy.[3]

For these reasons, as well as what the Catholic Church teaches about intercessory prayer, I believe that our prayers for the dying can unleash protection and mercy for those who are most in need of

God's mercy, especially at their moment of death.

Death is one of those times when the dying and the living are most open to the divine intervention, believer and non-believer alike. Witnessing death has a profound impact on us. We loathe our mortality and crave immortal life beyond the grave. Prayer is our attempt to become one with God; it fortifies us to walk into eternity with trust and joy.

***

I have experienced the providential care and the bountiful, unmerited mercy of God all through my life, even when I shut the door in the Lord's face. It is easier to recognize the saving hand of God as a believer. He provided me with multiple chances to begin anew through the power of His grace, forgiveness, and the sacraments—all undeserved instruments of His unfathomable Catholic Church

We may think that we are beyond the reach of Divine Mercy because of a "grave lack of discretionary judgment," a loving way of saying mortal sin without judging the state of a soul. I have found that the Catholic Church bends over backward to reconcile repentant sinners with the Lord.

The ecclesiastical annulment process extends the merciful arms of the Church to fallen away Catholics due to remarriage outside the Church. There are indeed no guarantees of a positive outcome, and the process takes time, work, humility, and patience, but the hope of reconciliation and peace is well worth the effort.

At Pentecost, Jesus sent the Holy Spirit to invigorate and sustain His mystical body, the Church. Jesus has left us with His very Real Presence in the Eucharist and the rest of the sacraments—the sacred CPR—to nurse us back to spiritual health. And through the Divine Mercy of a God smitten with us, the resurrection of the body and the life everlasting is a reality for us, sinners that we are.

I have a great devotion to the Divine Mercy of God. I invite you to pray the Divine Mercy Chaplet with me every day for the rest of your life in gratitude that you know Him and in intercession for those who don't yet know Him, especially for those who have lost hope and bought into the lie that they are beyond the mercy of God.

CHAPTER 3

THE GREATER THE SINNER

The focus of this book is Divine Mercy, an infinitely large topic for a skinny little book like this, and a topic too deep and mysterious for any human mind to grasp fully.

So, why have I written this book? Because Divine Mercy saved my life, and it can save yours and those of your loved ones.

But fear not, this book isn't an esoteric theological treatise on Divine Mercy. I am not qualified to write such an exposition. My primary qualification to write this book is that I am a sinner—a big one—and for way too long, an unrepentant sinner. My sins, once forgiven through the mercy of Jesus, were a window into the unconditional love of a faithful God, who never looked back. My credentials are well summarized by,

> *Therefore, I tell you, her sins, which were many, have been forgiven; hence she has shown great love. But the one to whom little is forgiven, loves little.* (Lk 7:47, NRSV)

When I accepted the reality of Jesus Christ and the truth of the Gospel, I had to admit that I was wrong about many things. My lousy, stupid choices reeked of selfishness and were more than wrong—some were mortally sinful. The blind, single-minded pursuit of my happiness and self-reliance spawned numerous causalities. No sin is personal; it always harms others. Sin had grown deep roots in the soil of my life. Lots of work was needed (and still is) to rework and replant that soil with selfless virtue.

Admitting my grievous sins and owning their destructive wake was a humbling experience. My process of making amends to others, while freeing, was nevertheless painful, especially when I wasn't forgiven or I was told, "People don't change." However, the process of "recovery" from the wages of sin in my pursuit to follow Christ was life-changing, and I wouldn't forego any of it, especially given the good that God brought out of it.

What had changed in my life? I experienced the unconditional Love and Divine Mercy of Jesus Christ through my conversion experience and my eventual return to the Catholic Church.

Soon after my conversion experience, my Christian counselor compared me to the outcast Samaritan woman at the well:

> *"Jesus said to her, 'Go, call your husband, and come back.' The woman answered him, 'I have no husband.' Jesus said to her, 'You are right in saying, "I have no husband"; for you have had five husbands, and the one you have now is not your husband. What you have said is true!'"* (Jn 4:16-18, NRSV).

Years ago, I felt judged by my counselor's analogy. The sting of that perceived judgment arose from my pride. I've since realized that most of my hurt had its roots in pride. Humility is the opposite of pride and spawns a resiliency to both valid or undeserved criticism.

There was a non-defensive, emotionally healthy way to view my counselor's comparison. Instead of identifying with the sins of the Samaritan woman, I could have identified with Jesus's unsolicited actions towards her. He came looking for her!

Christ had sought the Samaritan woman out in the heat of the day when they could be alone. He'd sent his apostles into town and then proceeded to minister to her broken, hardened heart. Her past sins did not make the Samaritan woman any less lovable to Jesus; instead, her sins made her a prime target of His Divine Mercy.

> ***The greater the sinner, the greater the right he has to My mercy.*** (*Diary*, 720)

Jesus offered the Samaritan woman the living water of rebirth and joy to replace her shackles of shame and slavery to sin. That is what Jesus does. He frees us to fall deeply in love with Him, whereby we attach more to Him and less to ourselves. We stop hiding our inherent brokenness from Him and others, and thereby diffuse the power of shame over our lives and neutralize one of Satan's favorite tools of destruction.

When we own our sins and fully recognize the undeserved forgiveness and mercy of Love Incarnate, there is no choice but to sing the praises of God—forever!

But there's more. In the book, *Conversion*, Fr. Donald Haggerty says that it would be a mistake to consider the fruit of God's mercy as only a salve that removes the shame of our sins and grants us forgiveness from our sins.[1]

The mercy of God is inseparable from the Paschal Sacrifice.[2] For this very reason, many saints recommended meditating on the passion and death of Our Lord.[3] They joined their sufferings to the passion of Christ.

> *By his passion and death on the cross Christ has given a new meaning to suffering: it can henceforth configure us to him and unite us with his redemptive Passion. (CCC 1505)*

It is both a great mystery and gift to participate, as the body of Christ, by uniting our suffering to the Son's passion. Redemptive suffering is a very Catholic facet of Christianity.[4] When we understand the tremendous cost of our salvation and the fount of God's mercy, our hunger, for intimacy with Christ, increases exponentially.

We fall in love with God for who HE is—not for what He can do for us. It is why obeying His commands becomes a light yoke and an easy burden. We learn to trust that He knows us better than we know ourselves, and agree to go by His playbook, the Bible.

Only through our union with Jesus Christ, through the Holy Spirit, can we know the Father, and be united with the Trinity in eternity. Being in perfect communion with the Trinity, through the body of Christ, is why God created us. We are only at peace when we rest in Him. As St. Augustine wrote,

> *You have made us for Yourself, and our heart is restless until it rests in You.*[5]

Why is the Divine Mercy Chaplet so powerful? Through the *Diary* of St. Faustina, Jesus gives us His very own words to offer His Paschal Sacrifice back to the Father. In exchange, we implore the Father to pour out healing Divine Mercy upon us and the whole world.

The Paschal Mystery is God the Father's plan for our salvation revealed through the God the Son, incarnated in the God-Man, Jesus Christ. Christ's unconditional love for us and the perfect union of His will to the Father's will, through the action of the Holy Spirit, is demonstrated most dramatically in the Paschal Sacrifice—Christ's passion and death on the Cross.

The Gospel accounts of the spiritual, emotional, and physical passion of Christ, mince no words. To approach divinity, we must pass through the door of Christ's sacred humanity, and this is most tangible in His passion and death.[6]

There is nothing that we can offer to the Father that can equal or exceed the pleasing fragrance of His Son's Paschal Sacrifice. Christ's sacrifice declares the eternal truth that love is inseparable from sacrifice. Love "done" well hurts; just ask God.

In the Sacrifice of the Mass, the priest commemorates and presents the entire Paschal Mystery anew. Jesus comes to be with us in a real way in His Eucharistic Presence. When we receive Him in Holy Communion in a state of grace, He is incorporated into every cell of our body. The Eucharistic banquet allows us to drink the "fruit" of Divine Love and, it is why we are Catholic.

While we may not be able to attend Mass and receive the Eucharist each day, we can pray the Divine Mercy Chaplet daily. In doing so, we offer God the Father, his Son's Paschal Sacrifice, in reparation for our sins. We beg the Father for mercy for us and the whole world in remembrance of Christ's sorrowful passion. Jesus encouraged St. Faustina to pray the Divine Mercy Chaplet nonstop for the conversion of sinners.

When we meditate on the passion of the Son, *we will love Him* [the Father] *with a love which finds, like the love of Jesus did, its crowning glory in the cross in Christ's sacrifice, which we should offer at every moment unceasingly to the Father, one with that Divine Redeemer."* [7]

Jesus told St. Faustina nothing pleased Him more than her meditating on His sorrowful passion and that it was the key to learning authentic humility.[8] A crucified God is the epitome of humility; an eternity isn't long enough to plumb the depths of that kind of humility. Jesus wants nothing more than to please the Father. If the Paschal Sacrifice is the most pleasing offering to the Father, then meditating on the Son's sorrowful passion would be very pleasing to Jesus, whose will is one with the Father.

St. John Paul II connects holiness and justice, through the conduit of Christ's passion and cross, to unveil unbridled love and mercy in his encyclical, *Dives in Misericordia,* delivered in Rome on November 30, 1980:

> *Christ, as the man who suffers really and in a terrible way in the Garden of Olives and on Calvary, addresses Himself to the Father—that Father whose love He has preached to people, to whose mercy He has borne witness through all of His activity.*
>
> *But He is not spared—not even He—the terrible suffering of death on the cross: "For our sake God made him to be sin who knew no sin,"(2 Cor. 5:21)...Indeed this Redemption is the ultimate and definitive revelation of the holiness of God, who is the absolute fullness of perfection: fullness of justice and of love, since justice is based on love, flows from it and tends towards it.*
>
> *In the passion and death of Christ-in the fact that the Father did not spare His own Son, but "for our sake made him sin"* [2 Cor. 5:21] - *absolute justice is expressed, for Christ undergoes the passion and cross because of the sins of humanity. This constitutes even a "superabundance" of justice, for the sins of man are "compensated for" by the sacrifice of the Man-God.*
>
> *Nevertheless, this justice, which is properly justice "to God's measure," springs completely from love: from the love of the Father and of the Son, and completely bears fruit in love. Precisely for this reason the divine justice revealed in the cross of Christ is "to God's measure," because it springs from love and is accomplished in love, producing fruits of salvation.*
>
> *The divine dimension of redemption is put into effect not only by bringing justice to bear upon sin, but also by restoring to love that creative power in man* [...by] *which he once more has access to the fullness of life and holiness that come from God.*
>
> *In this way, redemption involves the revelation of mercy in its fullness.*[9]

I trust in the power and promises of Divine Mercy. I hope to motivate you to join those of us who pray the Divine Mercy Chaplet daily and to provide additional bead-by-bead resources for your daily meditations.

PART TWO – HISTORICAL

© Thoom / Shutterstock.com

"Souls who spread the honor of My mercy I shield through their entire life as a tender mother her infant, and at the hour of death I will not be a Judge for them, but the Merciful Savior." *(Diary, 1075)*

CHAPTER 4

ST. FAUSTINA'S ROLE

St. Maria Faustina Kowalska of the Blessed Sacrament became one of my favorite saints after I finished her *Diary* in the Spring of 2012. I had yet to read in-depth biographies like those written by Maria Tarnawaska[1] or Ewa K. Czaczkowska[2]—both of which I highly recommend.

Who was this woman that recorded thirteen years of intimate conversations with Jesus and visions of Him written over four years? If St. Faustina was to be one of my best "girlfriends" in heaven, I wanted to know everything about her, just like I know about my best girlfriends here on earth.

St. Faustina was born Helena Kowalska in Glogowiec, a small rural village located slightly over 100 miles northwest of Lodz, the third-largest city in Poland. Born on August 25, 1905, Helena (or Helenka as a youngster) was the third of eight surviving children born to Marianna (nee Babel) and Stanislaus Kowalski.

The Kowalski family struggled to eke out a living on a few acres of exhausted soil with a cow or two. Stanislaus accepted odd carpentry jobs, using the inside of their tiny house as his shop in the winter to help feed his family. Food was not plentiful for the family, nor was the most basic clothing. Both parents were devout in their Catholic faith.

Although Helena would have preferred to attend daily Mass even as a young child, her daily chores and the distance of the closest Catholic church in the neighboring town made that infrequent. On Sundays, a single dress that rotated among the three oldest girls determined who would attend Mass.

Marianna readily admitted that Helena was the favorite child due to her responsible, obedient, and agreeable personality. Helena's siblings didn't seem to hold her parents' favoritism against her as they benefitted from the kindness of Helena, too. Sometimes Helena took her siblings' punishment, which further secured their affection.

Helena was a joyful child with light gray-green eyes and reddish hair. She possessed a highly sensitive nature and perceptive temperament. More religious than other children her age, Helena felt called to a perfect way of life during a Vespers service when she was only seven years old.

At the age of nine, Helena received her First Communion. When she walked home from the church afterward, a neighbor later recalled asking Helena why she was walking home alone without the company of the other village children. Helena reported she wasn't alone; Jesus was with her.

Helena started primary school late and aged out of the educational system at age twelve—after a mere three years. But it's likely Helena already knew how to read as her father, Stanislaus, was one of only two people in Glogowiec who knew how to read. He would have taught Helena to read using the few religious books that were available to them.

To call Helena Kowalska uneducated is a bit misleading. While she had only three years of formal education, Helena was an avid reader and possessed a sharp intellect and a fantastic memory. Even twenty-five years after her death, sisters in her religious order remembered her uncanny memory for details, which made it easy for Helena to learn new tasks.

At sixteen, Helena left home to work as a live-in domestic servant in Aleksandrow Lodzki. Such was the fate of at least four other sisters—with one younger sister hired out at age nine—as was commonly done by low-income families without money for dowries. Accommodations for food and board were typically minimal, with the majority of small wages given to their parents.

The following year, 1922, Helena returned home to announce that she desired to enter a convent. Helena had never met a religious sister and knew nothing of the differences between active and contemplative orders or that a particular charism that defined an order's mission.

Her parents were vehemently opposed as they had other plans for their daughter that included continuing to work as a domestic servant until she married. Helena, however, wanted to devote her life to Christ.

In the fall of 1922, Helena left home once again, this time to Lodz, and moved in with her uncle's family until she found employment first in a bakery and then working as domestic help for the next year and a half.

It was during her time in Lodz while attending a dance with one of her sisters, who also worked in the same town, that Helena had a vision of Jesus. Scourged and stripped of His garments, He asked Helena how long she would keep putting Him off.[3]

She left the dance soon after that and withdrew to the Cathedral of Saint Stanislaus Kostka, which still stands. Falling prostrate before the Blessed Sacrament in prayer that very evening, she received direction to go to Warsaw and enter a convent.[4]

She left soon after that vision and telling her sister in Lodz goodbye. Her uncle took an emotional Helena to the train station. She left for Warsaw with only that tiny bit of instruction: a convent located in Warsaw. The day after her arrival, the kindly pastor of St. James's Parish in a suburb in Warsaw listened to her story and helped her find employment and lodging with Aldona Lipszyc, with whom she would remain a life-long friend.

Helena endured many disappointing trips into Warsaw before she found a convent that would allow her entry. Finally, she knocked at the door of the Congregation of the Sisters of Our Lady of Mercy. After being assessed as "nothing special," she was told that if she earned money for her habit that the mother superior would accept her.

Approximately a year later, on August 1, 1925, Helena walked through the convent door on Zytnia Street with the required money for her clothing. Within two weeks, the mother superior sent the now postulate Helena away for two weeks to regain her strength. Helena's fragile health was already evident.

Helena had no idea what the charism of the Congregation of the Sisters of Our Lady of Mercy—she was just thrilled that any order would accept her. The charism of the Sisters of Our Lady of Mercy was to rehabilitate poor, uneducated women of ill-repute. These women had turned to the streets as their only source of livelihood. Poverty and hunger were rampant in Poland at the time.

The young girls and women—called wards—were given moral instruction and schooled in a domestic skill whereby they could earn a living, for example, as a seamstress.

The order had a first and second choir. The religious sisters who had the most education and entered with dowries comprised the first choir. The first choir taught the wards religion and their new occupational skill. Helena belonged to the second choir, which performed the work necessary to support the mission of the order, such as cooking, cleaning, gardening, everything but teaching the wards. Prayer time and retreats, and recreation were independent of the choir level.

Throughout her religious life, Helena often worked with the wards in the execution of her daily chores. They loved her kindness, and patience, even if they did find some of her habits, like praying cruciform on the pantry floor, a bit eccentric. And while it is true that the choir-level impacted how some sisters interacted with Sr. Faustina, it was not by design as odd as the arrangement sounds to us today. The order eventually did away with the two choirs sometime after Sr. Faustina's death.

During her postulancy, which was no more than nine months, Helena struggled to conform to convent life within the Congregation of the Sisters of Our Lady of Mercy. Even though Helena had an intensely rich interior life, she was not immune to the struggles of any other postulant. By the end of the first month, Helena confessed to her friend and ex-employer, Aldona Lipszyc, that she'd entered the wrong order. However, Jesus reassured Helena that she was in the exact convent in Warsaw that He had selected.

Helena finished her postulancy and began her novitiate in Krakow. In April of 1926, she received her veil and habit along with her new name Sr. Maria Faustina. At this time, she made her temporary profession of vows.

By Spring of 1927, Sr. Faustina was deeply immersed in a period of intense spiritual loneliness and torture, her "dark night of the soul." However, it was during this period that mystical graces inundated her soul, and her spiritual betrothal to Jesus took place. She was formally assigned to the convent in Krakow for not quite three years.

After her time in Krakow, Sr. Faustina was transferred to many different convents until her death. Table 1, on the next page, lists nine convents in the space of thirteen years between August 1925 and her death in October 1938. The psychological and physical impact of such frequent reassignments was a burden for Sr. Faustina.

Each convent had its distinct micro-culture: a different mother superior and confessor and community of religious women to integrate into—besides a different geographical locale.

Start Date	Location	Count	Approx. Time
Aug 1, 1925	Warsaw-Zynthia	1	2.6 weeks
Jan 23, 1926	Krakow	2	2.8 years
Oct 31, 1928	Warsaw-Zynthia	1	4 months
Feb 21, 1929	Vilnius	3	4 months
Jun 11, 1929	Warsaw-Grochow	4	8 months
Jul 7, 1929	Kiekrz	5	2 months
May-Jun 1930	Plock (*& Biala)	6,7	2.5 years
May 1932	Warsaw-Zynthia	1	3 weeks
Nov 1932	Walendow	8	4 days
Apr 18, 1933	Krakow	2	4.2 months
May 25, 1933	Vilnius	3	2.8 years
Mar 25, 1936	Walendow	8	6 weeks
May 1936	Derdy	9	4 days
May 12, 1936	Krakow	2	2.9 years

Table 1: *Sr. Faustina's convent assignments from her postulancy to her death on October 5, 1938, with the approximate length of stay in each convent. Sr. Faustina's frequent reassignments and moves were a trial for her. Data are compiled from various sources.*[5]

The multiple reassignments transpired while Sr. Faustina was desperately trying to understand her own spiritual life and the requests that the Lord was asking of her—which were especially difficult when those demands reached outside herself and required action by other people.

Since each new convent had a new mother superior and confessor, Sr. Faustina had to explain her interior life all over again. Some superiors and confessors were sympathetic or supportive of her inner spirituality, while others were put off by her claimed mystical experiences.

There were many times that Sr. Faustina did not trust her inner visions and voices, so she especially required guidance and constancy of a spiritual advisor who trusted her sanity and with whom she could be entirely honest.

Some of the religious sisters had little tolerance for Sr. Faustina's ways, while other sisters loved her and admired her wisdom and spirituality. Those critical of her were irritated by things they didn't understand, as is often the case in human interactions lacking in charity and looking to find fault.

Her detractors viewed Sr. Faustina as secretive. She asked for extra prayer time in the chapel, which some in her community felt detracted from her chores. Sisters observed Sr. Faustina crying during community prayer time. Sr. Faustina didn't hesitate to correct other sisters, even in the first choir, when their actions were "not pleasing to Jesus."

Through the emotional pain of being misunderstood or characterized as a hysteric, Sr. Faustina shared as little as possible with others about her interior life, the exception being what she needed to share with her mother superiors. Through her deep interior life and spiritual detachment, she developed a distinct and almost tangible "otherness" that was observed by her fellow sisters, some with disdain. Sr. Faustina never turned to people for comfort or support, only to Jesus. She didn't hold grudges or feel antipathy toward her detractors; she prayed for them.

Her many supervisors had a deep admiration of Sr. Faustina's interior life except for two. One supervisor in Plock had trouble with Sr. Faustina when she learned of Jesus's request to paint the image in Plock, and a second supervisor in Vilnius didn't understand her piety/interior life. But all her mother superiors admired her tremendous devotion to the Blessed Sacrament and Eucharistic adoration, and prayer, in general.

It is unknown when Sr. Faustina contracted tuberculosis. Her health had never been robust. She received a definitive diagnosis in 1934 after years of fatigue, generalized illness, inability to eat or to hold down food, fevers, and horrendous suffering. By this time of the diagnosis, her tuberculosis was advanced and had spread to her intestines. Sadly, because her diagnosis took so long, many of her sisters in the convent felt she was a hypochondriac.

As her body wasted away, her soul became as polished gold through her redemptive suffering. She experienced more prolonged periods of mystical union with God. It became clear that Sr. Faustina was dying in 1937, and sometime during that year, she achieved a permanent divinizing union of her soul with God.

Sr. Faustina was in and out of medical facilities/hospitals during the last several years of her life. She had a significant spiritual impact on the medical staff who cared for her. At times when she could barely walk from her widespread tuberculosis, she would drag herself out of bed to keep a vigil at the bedside of a dying patient. Eventually, she was forbidden to leave her room by her medical attendants.

She wrote of being transported to the bedside of several dying individuals in need of prayer. She was able to see the struggle in the spiritual realm for the soul of the terminally ill person. She also reported visitations from a deceased sister from her community in purgatory, asking for prayers. Sr. Faustina was able to read souls on occasion as to whether they were in a state of grace.

The Christian witness she was able to give during the slow, painful death that God has ordained for her is perhaps the most exceptional testimony of her unitive state with the Lord. On March 29, 1934, she wrote an act of offering her life for those sinners who had lost trust in Divine Mercy.[6]

When her pain was nothing short of anguish, she had the amazing ability to speak, smile, and pray not just for those in purgatory, as she had done earlier in her life, but for the poor sinner who refused to accept the mercy of Jesus.

Sr. Faustina met three priests who, over time, believed that the Lord was leading this humble sister to an extraordinary communion with Him and had been given a unique mission by Christ. Fr. Edmund Elter, S.J., was the very first to confirm the divine nature of her visions during a retreat in mid-1932. Next was Fr. Josef Andrasz, S.J., in the first half of 1933. After she took her permanent vows on May 1, 1933, Sr. Faustina met Fr. Michael Sopocko in June of 1933.

Fr. Sopocko was very busy with advanced studies when he first met Sr. Faustina in the confessional at the convent in Vilnius. (Vilnius at that time was part of Poland although now it is part of Lithuania.) He arranged to have her examined by a psychiatrist who pronounced her mental faculties as sound. Due to Fr. Sopocko's demanding schedule, he instructed Sr. Faustina to write down her conversations with Jesus and her spiritual life, in general, in a notebook. He was dumbstruck at the profound knowledge that this simple, meek sister had of theological matters.

The notebook was a further cause of deprecation by some sisters in her religious community; consequently, Sr. Faustina tried to hide her journaling. When caught in the act, she would demure that she was jotting down matters of conscience.

What started with a simple notebook grew to six journals—her now-famous *Diary*. Fr. Sopocko admits to some doubt concerning Sr. Faustina's interior life, although he still worked to help her obey the commands of the Lord. When Fr. Sopocko visited her two weeks before her death, he reported seeing her in ecstasy and that he had no more doubts about anything that she had told him, even receiving the Eucharist from angels.

Part of the challenge of reading the *Diary* is that Sr. Faustina destroyed her first version of Notebook 1 during a time of temptation. Fr. Sopocko was away in Rome when she burned the first version. She later recognized her mistake, and upon his return, Fr. Sopocko instructed her to rewrite what she had destroyed.

All six notebooks, comprising her *Diary*, were written over the last four years of Sr. Faustina's life while living in Vilnius and Krakow convents. As displayed in Table 2, her recreated Notebook 1 was her lengthiest and was composed over the most extended period, sixteen months. The six notebooks differed considerably in length and the number of months of their composition. Sr. Faustina never crossed anything out in her notebooks and used the convention of underlining the words of Jesus.

Her health continued to deteriorate, yet she continued journaling. Her last entry in Notebook VI was in June 1938, five months before her death. She just stopped writing with no indication that it would be her last entry. She was likely too sick to continue.

Notebook	Start date	Convent	Pages	*Diary* percent	Months
I – ver. 2	07/28/1934	Vilnius	217	35	16
II	11/24/1935	Vilnius	159	26	15
III	03/01/1937	Krakow	59	9	5
IV	08/10/1937	Krakow	29	5	1
V	10/20/1937	Krakow	88	14	4
VI	02/10/1938	Krakow	70	11	5

Table 2: *How the notebooks map into the Diary of Sr. Faustina. Notebook I is the second version (retrospective) after she destroyed the original text.*[7]

Present and retrospective events can be difficult to disentangle from undated entries in the journal. A detailed study by Fr. Jerzy (George) Mrówczyński and subsequent organization by Fr. Donald Calloway, MIC identifies with some certainty which *Diary* entries Sr. Faustina wrote retrospectively and which she wrote in the present rather than from memory.[8]

Table 3 maps the entries of Sr. Faustina's *Diary* into the year that she is writing (represented) and indicates whether she is writing about the past (retrospectively) or in the present based on the vital work of Fathers Mrowczynski and Calloway.

Notebook	Paragraph Nos.	Year Represented	Remarks
#1	7-39	1925	retrospective
#1	40-46	1929	retrospective
#1	47-54	1931	retrospective
#1	55-63	1933	retrospective
#1	64-84	1928	retrospective
#1	85-161	1934	started rewrite
#1	164-272	1933	retrospective
#1	273-351	1934	current year
#1	352-521	1935	current year
#2	522-584	1935	current year
#2	585-858	1936	current year
#2	859-1000	1937	current year
#3	1001-1230	1937	current year
#4	1231-1321	1937	current year
#5	1322-1448	1937	current year
#5	1449-1589	1938	current year
#6	1590-1803	1938	current year

Table 3: *Mapping Diary entries into Sr. Faustina's represented time frame: retrospective, or current. Data presented is the work of Fr. Jerzy Mrowczynski and subsequent organization by Fr. Donald Calloway.*[9]

The prophetic mission of Sr. Faustina began around mid-1933 during her time in the Vilnius convent. Before then, the Lord was directing her inner spiritual growth through all manner of hardships. Those struggles ultimately detached Sr. Faustina from her own sensitive nature. The result was a singular attachment to the Lord and His requests of her.

Her uncanny ability to withstand and unite her physical, emotional, and spiritual suffering was honed during this time of spiritual courtship and mentoring with Our Lord. Her *Diary* tracks this evolution in her spiritual growth most profoundly.

Sr. Faustina predicted the difficulty that her message of Divine Mercy would encounter initially and before being released into the whole world. She predicted certain events on the day of her canonization with uncanny specificity.

In February of 1931, over two years before her perpetual vows, Sr. Faustina had her first vision of the Merciful Jesus. Jesus requested that she have an image painted as she saw Him. Having no skill in painting and finding none in her community of sisters, Sr. Faustina begged Fr. Sopocko to help her execute this request of Jesus.

Fr. Sopocko arranged for her to meet with an artist who lived in his building, Eugeniusz Kazimirowski. Several times a week, her mother superior escorted Sr. Faustina to the painter's work area until the canvas was finished.

The painting was a massive disappointment to Sr. Faustina because it lacked the beauty of her vision. However, Jesus assured her that it was acceptable and would be a vehicle of great mercy for many souls. Eventually, the painting was displayed in a church in Vilnius, although its technical merits were criticized by many. Nonetheless, the Polish people cherished the portrait and other versions of the image painted over time. Adolf Hyla created the most popular version of the Merciful Jesus five years after Sr. Faustina's death under the direction of Fr. Josef Andrasz. Fr. Andrasz was Sr. Faustina's second confessor and the priest who administered the last rites to her.

Jesus also requested to have the Feast of Divine Mercy added to the liturgical calendar on the first Sunday after Easter. Such a task was beyond Sr. Faustina's ability. Still, through Fr. Sopocko's efforts and eventually, through the election of Cardinal Karol Wojtyla to the Papacy as Pope John Paul II, the adoption of this Feast did indeed come to pass 65 years after her death.

In September of 1935, Sr. Faustina was taught the Divine Mercy Chaplet by Jesus on her way into the convent chapel in Vilnius. Jesus instructed her to pray the Divine Mercy Chaplet nonstop. Her religious order already prayed a Chaplet of Mercy, but it was different than the one Jesus taught her. The Lord also instructed her on the specifics of a novena whence she was to pray the Divine Mercy Chaplet each of nine consecutive days with a different special intention each day.

Sr. Faustina wrote in her *Diary* about a new religious community devoted to Divine Mercy that Jesus wished to have founded. She initially thought that she was to start that community and spoke to her bishop about the new order in January 1937. By the time she received permission to leave her religious community to start the new one, in May 1937, she was too ill and realized that Jesus didn't require her to do this directly. That community, The Sisters of the Merciful Jesus, did begin in 1947 under the direction of Blessed Father Michael Sopocko.

Sr. Faustina died on October 5, 1938. She was thirty-three years old. The ravages of the disease that ended her short life had deformed her face and body. Her funeral was on October 7, 1938, on the first Friday of the month and the Feast of Our Lady of the Rosary. Her body was buried in the convent cemetery in Krakow. Her remains were transferred to their final resting place in Sanctuary of the Divine Mercy in Krakow-Lagiewniki on April 18, 1993.

Her *Diary* contains many entries where Sr. Faustina prayed that Poland would be spared great suffering for the ingratitude of her countrymen. Jesus told her if Poland was obedient to His will then it would become the spark that prepares the world for His final coming.[10]

The terrible war and hardships that Poland would suffer, predicted by Sr. Faustina, became a reality on September 1, 1939, when Germany invaded Poland starting World War II in Europe.[11] The Divine Mercy devotions introduced by Sr. Faustina's *Diary*, the images of the Merciful Jesus, the Chaplet of Divine Mercy, and the Novena quickly became popular in Poland, and later in the United States.

In 1958, the Holy Office in Rome, under Pope Pius XII, prepared a decree to permanently prohibit spreading the devotions, according to Sr. Faustina's revelations (referred to as the "cult" of Sr. Faustina). Unfortunately, a flawed translation of her notebooks was all the Holy Office had on which to base their evaluations, and the political situation in Poland complicated verification as well.

When the sisters of Our Lady of Mercy typed the text of Sr. Faustina's original six notebooks, some serious transcription errors and omissions were introduced. This typescript was then translated into Italian and French, retaining and perpetuating those mistakes.

Upon the death of Pope Pius XII, the next Pope, John XXIII, inherited this still-in-process decree of permanent prohibition of the "cult" of Sr. Faustina. Pope John XXIII changed the wording to call for only a temporary halt of the devotions until such a time that the Vatican's concerns could be addressed.

On October 21, 1965, Cardinal Karol Wojtyla began the informative process in the diocese of Krakow into the virtues and life of Sr. Maria Faustina Kowalska of the Blessed Sacrament—the first step toward sainthood. It was then that the journals were correctly transcribed and translated. The diocese of Krakow completed their research on September 20, 1967.

With the correct translations of the original documents in hand, the Sacred Congregation for the Doctrine of the Faith lifted the ban on the "cult" of Sr. Faustina on April 15, 1978. Sr. Faustina's prediction that all the Divine Mercy revelations would seem as lost for a while, but then would come to light, did indeed come to pass.[12]

Six months and one day later, on October 16, 1978, Cardinal Wojtyla was elected Pope John Paul II. Things moved very fast after that. In 1981 the first edition of the *Diary* was published; Sr. Faustina was beatified on April 18, 1993, and canonized on April 30, 2000—the first Sunday after Easter Sunday.[13] Pope John Paul II said that April 30, 2000, was the happiest day of his life.

My favorite quote from Pope John Paul II's homily on the day of St. Faustina's canonization follows:

> *It is this love* [human compassion and love when it takes the Love of God as its measure] *which must inspire humanity today, if it is to face the crisis of the meaning of life, the challenges of the most diverse needs and, especially, the duty to defend the dignity of every human person. Thus the message of divine mercy is also implicitly a message about the value of every human being. Each person is precious in God's eyes; Christ gave his life for each one; to everyone the Father gives his Spirit and offers intimacy.*
>
> *This consoling message is addressed above all to those who, afflicted by a particularly harsh trial or crushed by the weight of the sins they committed, have lost all confidence in life and are tempted to give in to despair. To them the gentle face of Christ is offered; those rays from his heart touch them and shine upon them, warm them, show them the way and fill them with hope. How many souls have been consoled by the prayer "Jesus, I trust in you," which Providence intimated through Sr Faustina! This simple act of abandonment to Jesus dispels the thickest clouds and lets a ray of light penetrate every life. Jezu, ufam Tobie* [Jesus I trust in You].[14]

On the very same day as St. Faustina's canonization, Pope John Paul II added Divine Mercy Sunday to the Catholic Church's liturgical calendar.

Although I gloss over the role of Fr. Michael Sopocko, now Blessed Michael Sopocko, and his heroic efforts to further the message of Divine Mercy as presented by St. Faustina, his role is worthy of an entire book.

The sequence of events that led to the Marian Fathers (of the Immaculate Conception of the BVM) to become caretakers of the Divine Mercy message and role of Cardinal Karol Wojtyla—later Pope John Paul II and now St. John Paul II—are other book-worthy efforts. I recommend the resources: *The Second Greatest Story Ever Told* by Michael E. Gaitley, MIC, and the DVD series, Divine Mercy and the Second Greatest Story Ever Told, which was produced by the Augustine Institute.

***

The Lord loves each of us more than we can imagine; after all, He created us to be with Him forever. His Son died to pay our passage into the eternal communion of love—the Trinity. We have only to obey His commandments and accept His mercy and forgiveness when we acknowledge our failures.

The life of St. Faustina testifies that in weakness, God manifests His strength. She offered her life as a victim soul[15] for people—sinners as we all are—and especially for those that have closed their hearts and minds to the Divine Mercy that God freely offers. St. Faustina may not be a girlfriend that I can hug, but she is one who understands the longings of a lost and searching heart, like mine was once, even before I did.

St. Faustina, pray for us!

CHAPTER 5

DIVINE MERCY DEVOTIONS

Through the *Diary* of St. Faustina, Jesus gives us five devotions or spiritual tools to help us pour out the blessings of Divine Mercy into our lives, those of our loved ones, and the whole world:

- Image of Merciful Jesus
- Feast of Divine Mercy
- Chaplet of Divine Mercy
- Novena of Divine Mercy Chaplets
- Hour of Divine Mercy

Fr. Ignatius Rozycki, who examined the *Diary* as part of the canonization process for St. Faustina, added a sixth element to the above list, "Sharing the Message of Divine Mercy." Bishop Robert Barron likes to remind his listeners that anyone in the Bible, who had an experience of God, was *always* given a mission.[1] If Divine Mercy has touched your life, then you have a mission to share the message!

One powerful way to proclaim the message is by sharing the impact Divine Mercy has had on your life. Our personal testimony is not a matter of debate and is rarely threatening, even to a skeptic. For example, communicating a reduction in anxiety when you pray the Divine Mercy Chaplet could crack open a window of opportunity—the Holy Spirit is always on the move. Another way to elicit interest is by sharing the fantastic promises that Jesus made to St. Faustina regarding the five devotions above.

Image of Divine Mercy (or Merciful Jesus)

On February 22, 1931, St. Faustina received a vision of Jesus while living at the convent in Plock, which happened to be a very challenging period in her life both spiritually and socially. Jesus told St. Faustina to paint an image according to the pattern that she saw with the words "Jesus, I trust in You." Our Lord said that through this image, many blessings would flow to souls. He requested that the painting be displayed first in the convent chapel and then the whole world.

> ***I promise that the soul that will venerate this image will not perish. I also promise victory over [its] enemies already here on earth, especially at the hour of death. I Myself will defend it as My own glory.*** (*Diary*, 48).

That image is known as the Divine Mercy Jesus or the Merciful Jesus. St. Faustina was never pleased with the finished canvas painted by Eugeniusz (Eugene) Kazimirowski because he had failed to capture the beauty of Jesus in her visions.

The original Divine Mercy image / Eugeniusz Marcin Kazimirowski (1934) / Holy Trinity Church in Vilnius, Lithuania / © Cezary Wojtkowski / Shutterstock.com

At the behest of her confessor, St. Faustina asked Jesus what the two rays emanating from His heart meant. Jesus explained that the red rays and pale rays represented the blood and water, respectively, that flowed from His pierced side at the crucifixion. The pale rays depict our sanctification (and purification in Baptism), and the blood represents our life (in Christ).[2]

The original painting has moved around plenty since its creation and now resides in the Holy Trinity Church (sometimes called the Shrine of Divine Mercy) in Vilnius, Lithuania.

The original Divine Mercy image has been an inspiration for many others. Adolph Hyla painted the most popular image in 1943 under the direction of Fr. Josef Andrasz, S.J., as shown on the front cover of this book. Critics and Clerics had decried Kazimirowski's image for lack of artistic balance, and the Hyla image because they felt Jesus looked too feminine.

However, Jesus cautioned not to belabor the details of the paint and brush strokes; instead what is important, are the graces that flow from the image. The Congregation of the Marian Fathers of the Immaculate Conception retains copyright on these images.[3]

Feast of Divine Mercy

During the homily at the canonization Mass of St. Faustina, April 30, 2000, St. Pope John Paul II declared that the first Sunday after Easter Sunday—also called the second Sunday of Easter—was to be celebrated universally as the Feast of Divine Mercy.

> *It is important then that we accept the whole message that comes to us from the word of God on this Second Sunday of Easter, which from now on throughout the Church will be called "Divine Mercy Sunday."*[4]

St. Faustina first wrote of Divine Mercy Sunday on February 22, 1931. Upon leaving the confessional, St. Faustina interiorly heard (again) that she was to paint the image of her vision of Jesus (the Divine Mercy Image) and to have it blessed on the first Sunday after Easter, which was to be called the Feast of Mercy (Divine Mercy Sunday).

The interior voice of Jesus came right after her confessor in Plock counseled her that Jesus merely wanted her to paint an image of Him on her soul. Fr. Sopocko and Fr. Andreaz, who were to become trusted spiritual directors for St. Faustina, were not yet her assigned confessors.

The Feast of [Divine] Mercy is mentioned many times in the *Diary*, and the special graces available on this Feast are mentioned three times in the *Diary*.[5] Among those references, Jesus makes tremendous promises to the faithful and sinners alike. Many have compared these graces to a second Baptism: complete forgiveness of sin and total cleansing of all temporal punishment due to sin.[6]

Although the Catholic Church has not formally ruled on the promises of Divine Mercy Sunday, she has ascertained that there is nothing opposed to the faith.

The extreme grace conferred on Divine Mercy Sunday is different than a plenary indulgence. A plenary indulgence is hard to receive as *perfect* contrition for sins is a requirement.[7] The grace associated with Divine Mercy Sunday only requires *imperfect* contrition. During the SARS-CoV-2 Virus Pandemic, Pope Frances announced an emergency plenary indulgence on Divine Mercy Sunday 2020.[8]

Various priests, including Fr. Ignatius Rozycki, provided guidance consistent with Our Lord's recorded words to St. Faustina: one must receive the sacrament of Penance before and close to Divine Mercy Sunday and then receive the Eucharist in a state of grace.[9]

Sixty-nine years after Jesus asked that the second Sunday after Easter be set aside as a Feast to Divine Mercy, Pope John Paul II declared it to be so according to St. Faustina's specifications.

Chaplet of Divine Mercy

On September 13, 1935, Jesus taught St. Faustina the Divine Mercy Chaplet. He promised great graces to those who pray the Divine Mercy Chaplet, especially at the hour of their death.[10] Our Lord was clear that the Divine Mercy Chaplet wasn't only a prayer for St. Faustina, but to be prayed by everyone. When we persist in humbly praying the Divine Mercy Chaplet, we perform a Spiritual Work of Mercy. The Divine Mercy Chaplet is a conduit to obtain anything consistent with the will of Jesus, which is in perfect union with that of the Father.

Our Lord recommended the Divine Mercy Chaplet as a last resort, even for those great sinners with hardened hearts.[11] Jesus promised that when we pray the Divine Mercy Chaplet at the bedside of a dying person that He will meet that person as the Merciful Savior rather than the Just Judge.[12]

It was for this reason that we prayed the Divine Mercy Chaplet at my father's bedside two days before he entered eternal life. He never regained consciousness, but I trust that this prayer increased his spiritual protection at the end of his life. Praying the Divine Mercy Chaplet with the dying is a crucial ministry in which we can all participate.

Divine Mercy Novena of Chaplets

In 1937, Jesus asked St. Faustina to make a Novena of Divine Mercy Chaplets on nine consecutive days. The first day of the novena was to begin on Good Friday and ninth day on the Saturday before Divine Mercy Sunday (the second Sunday of Easter).

Jesus asked St. Faustina to bring a different group of individuals to the fountain of His mercy on each of the nine days. The groups either comforted Jesus or intensified His suffering during His passion. St. Faustina composed beautiful prayers specific to each day. Her moving intercessions glorify the Lord, request graces to surmount the hardships of this life, and enfold them in God's boundless mercy.

The requests for each day of the Novena are listed below. The first paragraph notation from the *Diary* contains Christ's words; the subsequent paragraph notations include St. Faustina's prayers.

First Day – ***Today bring to Me all mankind, especially all sinners...*** (*Diary*, 1210; 1211)

Second Day – ***Today bring to Me the souls of priests and religious...*** (*Diary*, 1212;1213)

Third Day – ***Today bring to Me all devout and faithful souls...*** (*Diary*, 1214;1215)

Fourth Day – ***Today bring to Me the pagans*** [those who do not believe in God] ***and those who do not yet know Me...*** (*Diary*, 1216;1217)

Fifth Day – ***Today bring to Me the souls of heretics and schismatics*** [those who have separated themselves from the Church] ... (*Diary*, 1218; 1219)

Sixth Day – ***Today bring to Me the meek and humble souls and the souls of little children...*** (*Diary*, 1220; 1221, 1223)

Seventh Day – ***Today bring to Me the souls who especially venerate and glorify My mercy...*** (*Diary*, 1224; 1225)

Eighth Day – ***Today bring to Me the souls who are detained in [...] Purgatory...*** (*Diary*, 1226; 1227)

Ninth Day – ***Today bring to Me souls who have become lukewarm...*** (*Diary*, 1228; 1229)

When praying the Novena of Divine Mercy Chaplets, we can also include our special intentions, as did my friend, Blanche, when she prayed for my return to the Catholic Church.

Hour of Great Mercy

Three of the four Evangelists write that Jesus died during the three o'clock afternoon hour.[13] Jesus requested that during the hour of His death, St. Faustina immerse herself in His passion, especially for sinners, even if only for a moment.[14] My favorite quote regarding this hour of great mercy is,

> ***In this hour you can obtain everything for yourself and for others for the asking; it was the hour of grace for the whole world—mercy triumphed over justice.*** (*Diary*, 1572)

The above *Diary* entry assumes that we are asking for something consistent with God's will. Since God desires the salvation of all souls, this is a perfect time to pray for family and friends still lacking the gift of faith or who have died, for those who will die today, for all unrepentant sinners, and the souls in purgatory.

Many people elect to pray the Divine Mercy Chaplet during the three o'clock hour because of Christ's words to St. Faustina. If that time doesn't fit your schedule, pick a time that does, and establish a habit of prayer then. Any time is pleasing to the Lord—it is the three o'clock hour somewhere in the world.

Objections of Divine Mercy Devotions

Here I address several objections to the Divine Mercy Devotions that I have encountered. Perhaps the most virulent are those leveled against St. Faustina indirectly by charging that St. John Paul II canonized her because of their common Polish nationality.

Such unfortunate criticism detracts from the beauty of the Divine Mercy message. Some people object because the Church suppressed the *Diary* and the Divine Mercy devotions for almost twenty years. It's true that on March 6, 1959, a papal notification prohibited the spreading of the Divine Mercy Devotions in the forms expressed by Sr. Faustina in her *Diary*.

It's also true that on April 15, 1978, the Holy See revoked the prohibition entirely because the St. Faustina's religious order provided a new version of the *Diary* where they had fixed the original transcription errors and deletions. In 1981, with its publication, the public had access to the first edition of the corrected *Diary*.

Miracles for St. Faustina's Canonization

The two miracles required for St. Faustina's canonization received the same scrutiny as usual for any saint. The first miracle was the cure of Maureen Digan of western Massachusetts, USA.[15] Maureen had a severe and debilitating form of lymphedema, called Milroy disease, that left her crippled after the amputation of one leg and was soon expected to claim the other leg.

On March 28, 1981, Maureen and her husband, Bob, made a pilgrimage and prayed at the tomb of Sr. Faustina. Bob had a strong faith, whereas Maureen had lost her faith over the course of her illness that began at age fifteen.

When praying at Sr. Faustina's tomb, Maureen recalls challenging Faustina to "do something" as she had traveled a long way to make her petition. She heard an inner voice that invited her to ask for what she wanted. She did and had an immediate sensation of lessened pain, and her leg healed nearly immediately.

The second miracle, in 1995, was the healing of Fr. Ron Pytel from aortic valve stenosis that severely compromised the left ventricle of his heart.[16] His heart condition had not responded well to surgery. Through the intercession of then Blessed Faustina, in concert with a healing prayer group and a brother priest, he was able to achieve a healthy, normal heart as verified by his cardiologist.

***

The *Diary* has received a *NIHIL OBSTAT* and *IMPRIMATUR* from the Catholic Church authorities, which means that the *Diary* is free from moral or doctrinal error. However, it does not mean that the faithful are required to believe or agree with its contents. On the other hand, St. Faustina's canonization and the institution of the Feast of Divine Mercy on the first Sunday after Easter inspire a great deal of confidence in her revelations as recorded in her *Diary*.

After I read the *Diary*, my faith grew, especially in the Real Presence of the Eucharist, which was something that I had asked the Lord for upon my return to the Catholic Church between Easter Sunday and Divine Mercy Sunday in 2012.

The *Diary* has been a great gift to me. I encourage you to read the *Diary* directly, keeping in mind the historical context in which St. Faustina is writing. There is no substitute for reading the words of the saint directly.

PART THREE – PRAYERFUL

© *Thoom / Shutterstock.com*

Look into My Heart and see there the love and mercy which I have for humankind, and especially for sinners. Look, and enter into My Passion. (*Diary*, 1663)

CHAPTER 6

LOGISTICS OF THE DIVINE MERCY CHAPLET

Jesus made phenomenal promises to those who pray the Divine Mercy Chaplet, according to the *Diary* of St. Faustina. Jesus promised that those who recite this prayer would receive great mercy at the hour of their death. And amazingly, when prayed at the bedside of the dying, Christ will stand as the Merciful Savior (not the Judge) between the Father and the dying person.[1]

When I first read the *Diary*, I was just starting my journey back home to the Catholic Church. However, I immediately began praying the Divine Mercy Chaplet. My commitment to pray the Divine Mercy Chaplet was well before the Rosary became part of my daily prayer life. The *Diary* and the promises that Jesus made to St. Faustina regarding the graces of the Chaplet impacted me greatly.

I pray the Divine Mercy Chaplet on regular rosary beads. Analogous to the Rosary, there are introductory prayers, central prayers consisting of five decades, and concluding prayers. Several prayers at the beginning and the ending of the Chaplet, are considered optional because St. Faustina is the author—not Jesus. I include all the prayers in this chapter.

In her *Diary*, St. Faustina recorded that Jesus instructed her first to say three introductory prayers: *Our Father*, *Hail Mary*, and *The Apostles' Creed*.[2]

The central prayers of the Divine Mercy Chaplet, which correspond to the five decades of the Rosary, are two new prayers dictated by Jesus to St. Faustina. Continuing the Rosary analogy, I say *The Eternal Father*, in place of the *Our Father*, at the beginning of each decade of the chaplet; I recite the *For the Sake of His Sorrowful*

Passion, in place of the *Hail Mary*.

I repeat the concluding prayer, *Holy God,* three times, after the fifth decade, which was another new prayer dictated to St. Faustina by Jesus.

The form of the Divine Mercy Chaplet that I pray includes three additional optional prayers that St. Faustina composed. The Marian Fathers of the Immaculate Conception of the B.V.M have popularized the optional prayers through their excellent devotional materials.

I pray two of these optional prayers at the beginning of the Divine Mercy Chaplet (*You Expired, Jesus* followed by *O Blood and Water*); I pray the other prayer (*Eternal God*) after the thrice invoked *Holy God* prayer. See the diagram at the end of this chapter.

Prayers of the Divine Mercy Chaplet

Sign of the Cross

In the name of the Father and of the Son and of the Holy Spirit, Amen. (Note: Use the crucifix of the rosary to touch the forehead, the lower chest, the left shoulder, and then the right shoulder. At this point, I kiss the crucifix on my rosary; some people kiss the crucifix before or after they make the sign of the cross.)

Introductory Prayers

The optional prayers emphasize the connectedness of the Paschal Sacrifice with the outpouring of Divine Mercy. Many people include them in their Divine Mercy Chaplet, as do I.

You Expired, Jesus

You expired, Jesus, but the source of life gushed forth for souls, and the ocean of mercy opened up for the whole world. O Fount of Life, unfathomable Divine Mercy, envelop the whole world and empty Yourself out upon us. (*Diary*, 1319). (Optional)

O Blood and Water (Repeat three times.)

O Blood and Water which gushed forth from the Heart of Jesus as a fount of mercy for us, I trust in You! (*Diary*, 84) (Optional)

Our Father

Our Father, who art in heaven, hallowed be Thy name. Thy kingdom come: Thy will be done on earth as it is in heaven. Give us this day our daily bread. And forgive us our trespasses as we forgive those who trespass against us. And lead us not into temptation: but deliver us from evil. Amen.

Hail Mary *(traditional form)*

Hail Mary, full of grace, the Lord is with thee. Blessed art thou among women, and blessed is the fruit of thy womb, Jesus. Holy Mary, Mother of God, pray for us sinners, now and at the hour of our death. Amen.

Apostles' Creed

I believe in God, the Father Almighty, Creator of heaven and earth; and in Jesus Christ, his only Son, our Lord, who was conceived by the Holy Spirit, born of the Virgin Mary, suffered under Pontius Pilate, was crucified, died and was buried; he descended into hell; on the third day He rose again from the dead; he ascended into heaven, and is seated at the right hand of God the Father almighty; from there he will come to judge the living and the dead. I believe in the Holy Spirit, the Holy Catholic Church, the communion of saints, the forgiveness of sins, the resurrection of the body, and the life everlasting. Amen.

Central Prayers

The *Eternal Father* and *For the Sake of His Sorrowful Passion* comprise the central prayers. Jesus dictated both prayers to St. Faustina. As in all prayers that Jesus taught, He addresses God the Father. Since there are fifty repetitions of the *For the Sake of His Sorrowful Passion*, I use the meditation aids contained in Chapter 7 or Chapter 8.

Eternal Father

Eternal Father, I offer You the Body and Blood, Soul and Divinity of Your Dearly Beloved Son, Our Lord, Jesus Christ, in atonement for our sins and those of the whole world. *(Diary*, 476).

For the Sake of His Sorrowful Passion

For the Sake of His sorrowful Passion have mercy on us and on the whole world. (*Diary*, 476)

Concluding Prayers

The concluding prayers include the *Holy God* prayer, which Jesus dictated to St. Faustina, and optional *Eternal God* prayer, which she wrote.

Holy God (Repeat three times.)

Holy God, Holy Mighty One, Holy Immortal One, have mercy on us and on the whole world. (*Diary*, 476)

Eternal God

Eternal God in whom mercy is endless and the treasury of compassion inexhaustible, look kindly upon us and increase Your mercy in us, that in difficult moments I might not despair nor become despondent, but with great confidence submit ourselves to Your holy will, which is Love and Mercy itself. (*Diary*, 950) (Optional)

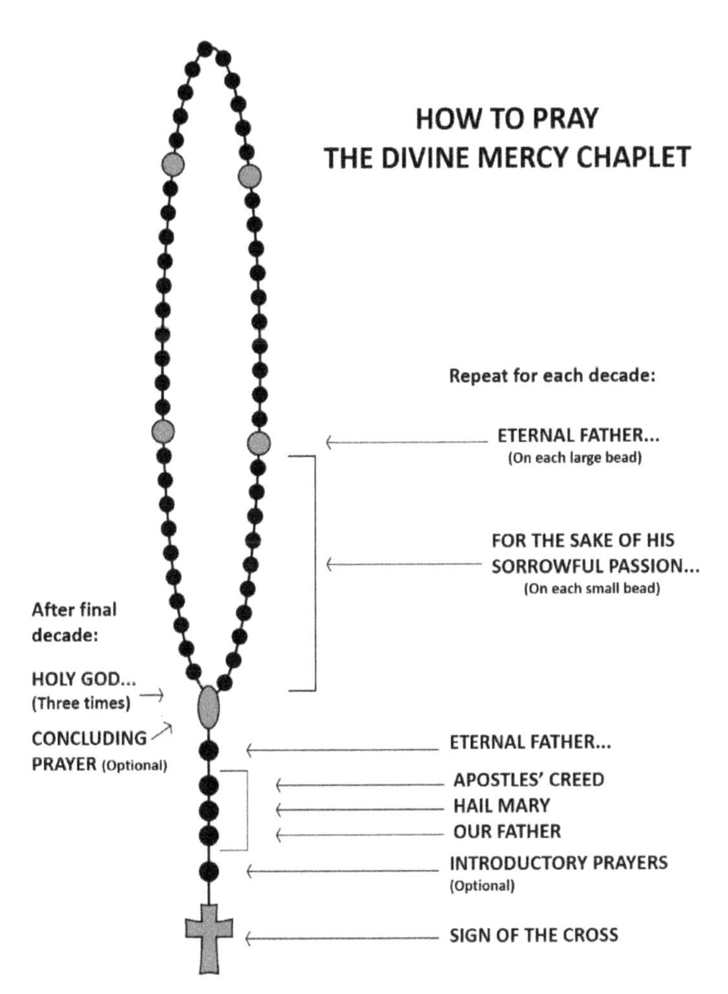

© Thoom / Shutterstock.com / modified by MKDaly

CHAPTER 7

SCRIPTURE & ART MEDITATIONS

This chapter partitions fifteen distinct events from the passion and death of Christ into three chronological sequences: I, II, III. I've selected these events because there are detailed New Testament accounts in at least one of the four Gospels. Each sequence corresponds to five decades of the Divine Mercy Chaplet; each decade couples a fine-art image with ten scriptural quotations.

On Good Friday 1991, St. John Paul II presented the Scriptural Stations of the Cross. He proposed them as a way to enhance our understanding, visualization, and meditation through the use of Scripture.[1]

There is a strong correspondence between the fifteen events that I have selected for meditation while praying the Divine Mercy Chaplet, and the fourteen events in St. John Paul II's Scriptural Stations of the Cross.

The first sequence of events with companion scriptural meditations for the Divine Mercy Chaplet is:

- **Decade 1. Thirty Pieces of Silver** – Jesus is betrayed by Judas for thirty pieces of silver.
- **Decade 2. Agony in the Garden** – Christ experiences the anguish of his impending betrayal, suffering, and death.
- **Decade 3. Kiss of Betrayal** – Judas leads the Jewish officials and soldiers to Christ, whom he betrays with a kiss.
- **Decade 4. Arrest of Christ** – Bound as a criminal, Christ is led away for mock trials.
- **Decade 5. Examination by Annas** – Jesus is questioned by the former high priest.

The second sequence of events with companion scriptural meditations for the Divine Mercy Chaplet is:

- **Decade 1. Denial by Peter** – Peter denies Christ, as predicted by Jesus earlier.
- **Decade 2. Trial Before Sanhedrin** – Caiaphas and the Sanhedrin decide that Christ must die for blasphemy.
- **Decade 3. Pilate Sends Jesus to Herod** – Pilate sends Christ to Herod, trying to avoid dealing with Him.
- **Decade 4. Jesus Stands Before Pilate** – Pilate declares that Christ has committed no capital crime and interrogates Christ about His kingship.
- **Decade 5. Crucify Him** – The priest and scribes inflame the crowd to demand the death of Christ and to set Barabbas free.

The third sequence of events with companion scriptural meditations for the Divine Mercy Chaplet is:

- **Decade 1. The Way to Calvary** – Scourged, crowned with thorns, and mocked, Jesus makes His way to the Cross.
- **Decade 2. Jesus Is Nailed to the Cross** – Our Lord is stripped and nailed to the cross between two thieves.
- **Decade 3. Jesus Hangs on the Cross** – Christ extends mercy to the repentant thief and gives His mother to the whole world.
- **Decade 4. Jesus Dies on the Cross** – In perfect submission to the will of the Father, Jesus gives up His Spirit.
- **Decade 5. Blood and Water Gush Forth** – The living fountain of Mercy opens up for the whole world.

SEQUENCE I –
SCRIPTURE & ART MEDITATIONS

- **Decade 1. Thirty Pieces of Silver** – Jesus is betrayed by Judas for thirty pieces of silver.
- **Decade 2. Agony in the Garden** – Christ experiences the anguish of his impending betrayal, suffering, and death.
- **Decade 3. Kiss of Betrayal** – Judas leads the Jewish officials and soldiers to Christ whom he betrays with a kiss.
- **Decade 4. Arrest of Christ** – Bound as a criminal, Christ is led away.
- **Decade 5. Examination by Annas** – Jesus is questioned by the former high priest.

Introductory Prayers

Sign of the Cross...

You expired, Jesus, *but the source of life gushed forth for souls, and the ocean of mercy opened up for the whole world. O Fount of Life, unfathomable Divine Mercy, envelop the whole world and empty Yourself out upon us.* (*Diary*, 1319) (Optional)

O Blood and Water, *which gushed forth from the Heart of Jesus as a fount of mercy for us, I trust in You!* (*Diary*, 187) (Repeat three times.) (Optional)

Our Father...

Hail Mary...

Apostles' Creed...

Decade 1. Thirty Pieces of Silver

Eternal Father, I offer You the Body and Blood, Soul and Divinity of Your Dearly Beloved Son, Our Lord, Jesus Christ, in atonement for our sins and those of the whole world. (*Diary*, 476)

On each "*Hail Mary*" bead, pray: ***For the sake of His sorrowful Passion, have mercy on us and on the whole world.*** (*Diary*, 476)

1. ***For the sake...*** As they were gathering in Galilee, Jesus said to them, "The Son of Man is going to be betrayed into human hands, (Mt 17:22, NRSV)

2. ***For the sake...*** and they will kill him, and on the third day he will be raised." And they were greatly distressed. (Mt 17:23, NRSV)

3. ***For the sake...*** Then one of the twelve, who was called Judas Iscariot, went to the chief priests (Mt 26:14, NRSV)

4. ***For the sake...*** and said, "What will you give me if I betray him to you?" They paid him thirty pieces of silver. (Mt 26:15, NRSV)

5. ***For the sake...*** When it was evening, he took his place with the twelve; (Mt 26:20, NRSV)

6. ***For the sake...*** and while they were eating, he said, "Truly I tell you, one of you will betray me." (Mt 26:21, NRSV)

7. ***For the sake...*** And they became greatly distressed and began to say to him one after another, "Surely not I, Lord?" (Mt 26:22, NRSV)

8. ***For the sake...*** He answered, "The one who has dipped his hand into the bowl with me will betray me." (Mt 26:23, NRSV)

9. ***For the sake...*** Judas, who betrayed him, said, "Surely not I, Rabbi?" He replied, "You have said so." (Mt 26: 25, NRSV)

The Last Supper / Carl Heinrich Bloch (c. 1865-1879) / Frederiksborg Palace, Hillerød, Denmark / Wikipedia Commons {PD-old-100}

10. ***For the sake...*** Jesus said to him, "Do quickly what you are going to do." So, after receiving the piece of bread, he immediately went out. And it was night. (Jn 13: 27b, 30, NRSV)

Decade 2. Agony in the Garden

Eternal Father, I offer you the Body and Blood, Soul and Divinity of Your Dearly Beloved Son, Our Lord, Jesus Christ, in atonement for our sins and those of the whole world. (*Diary*, 476)

On each "*Hail Mary*" bead, pray: ***For the sake of His sorrowful Passion, have mercy on us and on the whole world.*** (*Diary*, 476)

1. ***For the sake...*** Then Jesus went with them to a place called Gethsemane; and he said to his disciples, "Sit here while I go over there and pray." (Mt 26:36, NRSV)

2. ***For the sake...*** He took with him Peter and James and John, and began to be distressed and agitated. (Mk 14:33, NRSV)

3. ***For the sake...*** And he said to them, "I am deeply grieved, even to death; remain here, and keep awake." (Mk 14:34, NRSV)

4. ***For the sake...*** And going a little farther, he threw himself on the ground and prayed that, if it were possible, the hour might pass from him. (Mk 14:35, NRSV)

5. ***For the sake...*** He said, "Abba, Father, for you all things are possible; remove this cup from me; yet, not what I want, but what you want." (Mk 14:36, NRSV)

6. ***For the sake...*** Then he came to the disciples and found them sleeping; and he said to Peter, "So, could you not stay awake with me one hour?" (Mt 26:40, NRSV)

7. ***For the sake...*** Again he went away for the second time and prayed, "My Father, if this cannot pass unless I drink it, your will be done." (Mt 26:42, NRSV)

8. ***For the sake...*** Then an angel from heaven appeared to him and gave him strength. (Lk 22:43, NRSV)

Agony in the Garden / Francesco Trevisani (1740) / Kelvingrove Art Gallery and Museum, Glasgow, Scotland / Wikipedia Commons {PD-old-100}

9. ***For the sake...*** In his anguish he prayed more earnestly, and his sweat became like great drops of blood falling down on the ground. (Lk 22:44, NRSV)

10. ***For the sake...*** When he got up from prayer, he came to the disciples and found them sleeping because of grief[.] (Lk 22:45, NRSV)

Decade 3. Kiss of Betrayal

Eternal Father, I offer You the Body and Blood, Soul and Divinity of Your Dearly Beloved Son, Our Lord, Jesus Christ, in atonement for our sins and those of the whole world. (*Diary*, 476)

On each "*Hail Mary*" bead, pray: ***For the sake of His sorrowful Passion, have mercy on us and on the whole world.*** (*Diary*, 476)

1. ***For the sake...*** Then he came to the disciples and said to them, "Are you still sleeping and taking your rest? (Mt 26:45a, NRSV)

2. ***For the sake...*** See, the hour is at hand, and the Son of Man is betrayed into the hands of sinners. Get up, let us be going. See, my betrayer is at hand." (Mt 26:45b-46, NRSV)

3. ***For the sake...*** So Judas brought a detachment of soldiers together with police from the chief priests and the Pharisees, and they came there with lanterns and torches and weapons. (Jn 16:3, NRSV)

4. ***For the sake...*** Now the betrayer had given them a sign, saying, "The one I will kiss is the man; arrest him." (Mt 26:49, NRSV)

Kiss of Judas / Giotto (c. 1306) / Scrovegni (Arena) Chapel, Padua, Italy / Wikipedia Commons {PD-old-100}

5. ***For the sake...*** At once he came up to Jesus and said, "Greetings, Rabbi!" and kissed him. (Mt 26:50, NRSV)

6. ***For the sake...*** Then Jesus, knowing all that was to happen to him, came forward and asked them, "Whom are you looking for?" (Jn 16:4, NRSV)

7. ***For the sake...*** They answered, "Jesus of Nazareth." Jesus replied, "I am he." Judas, who betrayed him, was standing with them. (Jn 16:5, NRSV)

8. ***For the sake...*** When Jesus said to them, "I am he," they stepped back and fell to the ground. (Jn 16:6, NRSV)

9. ***For the sake...*** Again he asked them, "Whom are you looking for?" And they said, "Jesus of Nazareth." (Jn 17:7, NRSV)

10. ***For the sake...*** Jesus answered, "I told you that I am he. So if you are looking for me, let these men go." (Jn 17:8, NRSV)

Decade 4. Arrest of Christ

Eternal Father, I offer You the Body and Blood, Soul and Divinity of Your Dearly Beloved Son, Our Lord, Jesus Christ, in atonement for our sins and those of the whole world. (*Diary*, 476)

On each "*Hail Mary*" bead, pray: ***For the sake of His sorrowful Passion, have mercy on us and on the whole world.*** (*Diary*, 476)

1. ***For the sake...*** Then Jesus said to them, "You will all become deserters because of me this night; for it is written, 'I will strike the shepherd, and the sheep of the flock will be scattered.'" (Mt 26:31, NRSV)

2. ***For the sake...*** Then they came and laid hands on Jesus and arrested him. (Mt 26:50b, NRSV)

3. ***For the sake...*** Then Simon Peter, who had a sword, drew it, struck the high priest's slave, and cut off his right ear. The slave's name was Malchus. (Jn 16:10, NRSV)

4. ***For the sake...*** Jesus said to Peter, "Put your sword back into its sheath. Am I not to drink the cup that the Father has given me?" (Jn 16:11, NRSV)

Christ Taken Prisoner / Giuseppe Cesari (c. 1597) / Museumslandschaft Hessen Kassel, Germany / Wikipedia Commons {PD-old-100}

5. ***For the sake...*** But Jesus said, "No more of this!" And he touched his ear and healed him. (Lk 22:51, NRSV)

6. ***For the sake...*** "Do you think that I cannot appeal to my Father, and he will at once send me more than twelve legions of angels?" (Mt 26:53, NRSV)

7. ***For the sake...*** "But how then would the scriptures be fulfilled, which say it must happen in this way?" (Mt 26:54, NRSV)

8. ***For the sake...*** At that hour Jesus said to the crowds, "Have you come out with swords and clubs to arrest me as though I were a bandit?" (Mt 26:55a, NRSV)

9. ***For the sake...*** "Day after day I sat in the temple teaching, and you did not arrest me." (Mt 26:55b, NRSV)

10. ***For the sake...*** "But all this has taken place, so that the scriptures of the prophets may be fulfilled." Then all the disciples deserted him and fled. (Mt 26:56a, NRSV)

Decade 5. Examination by Annas

Eternal Father, I offer you the Body and Blood, Soul and Divinity of Your Dearly Beloved Son, Our Lord, Jesus Christ, in atonement for our sins and those of the whole world. (*Diary*, 476)

On each "*Hail Mary*" bead, pray: ***For the sake of His sorrowful Passion, have mercy on us and on the whole world.*** (*Diary*, 476)

1. ***For the sake...*** So the soldiers, their officer, and the Jewish police arrested Jesus and bound him. (Jn 18:12, NRSV)

2. ***For the sake...*** First they took him to Annas, who was the father-in-law of Caiaphas, the high priest that year. (Jn 18:13, NRSV)

3. ***For the sake...*** Caiaphas was the one who had advised the Jews that it was better to have one person die for the people. (Jn 18:14, NRSV)

4. ***For the sake...*** Then the high priest questioned Jesus about his disciples and about his teaching. (Jn 18:19, NRSV)

5. ***For the sake...*** Jesus answered, "I have spoken openly to the world; I have always taught in synagogues and in the temple, (Jn 18:20a, NRSV)

6. ***For the sake...*** where all the Jews come together. I have said nothing in secret. (Jn 18:20b, NRSV)

7. ***For the sake...*** Why do you ask me? Ask those who heard what I said to them; they know what I said." (Jn 18:21, NRSV)

8. ***For the sake...*** When he had said this, one of the police standing nearby struck Jesus on the face, saying, "Is that how you answer the high priest?" (Jn1 8:22, NRSV)

Jesus in the House of Annas / José de Madrazo y Agudo (1803) / Prado National Museum, Madrid / Wikipedia Commons {PD-old-100}

9. ***For the sake...*** Jesus answered, "If I have spoken wrongly, testify to the wrong. But if I have spoken rightly, why do you strike me?" (Jn 18:23, NRSV)

10. ***For the sake...*** Then Annas sent him bound to Caiaphas, the high priest. (Jn 18:24, NRSV)

Closing Prayers

Holy God*, *Holy Mighty One, Holy Immortal One, have mercy on us and on the whole world. (Repeat three times.) (*Diary*, 476)

Eternal God, *in whom mercy is endless and the treasury of compassion inexhaustible, look kindly upon us and increase Your mercy in us, that in difficult moments we might not despair nor become despondent, but with great confidence submit ourselves to Your holy will, which is Love and Mercy itself.* (*Diary*, 950) (Optional)

Sign of the Cross...

SEQUENCE II –
SCRIPTURE & ART MEDITATIONS

- **Decade 1. Denial by Peter** – Peter denies Christ, as predicted by Jesus earlier.
- **Decade 2. Trial Before Sanhedrin** – Caiaphas and the Sanhedrin decide Christ must die for blasphemy.
- **Decade 3. Pilate Sends Jesus to Herod** – Pilate sends Christ to Herod, trying to avoid dealing with Him.
- **Decade 4. Jesus Stands Before Pilate** – Pilate declares that Christ has committed no capital crime and interrogates Christ about His kingship.
- **Decade 5. Crucify Him** – The priest and scribes inflame the crowd to demand the death of Christ and to set Barabbas free.

Introductory Prayers

Sign of the Cross...

You expired, Jesus, *but the source of life gushed forth for souls, and the ocean of mercy opened up for the whole world. O Fount of Life, unfathomable Divine Mercy, envelop the whole world and empty Yourself out upon us.* (*Diary*, 1319) (Optional)

O Blood and Water, *which gushed forth from the Heart of Jesus as a fount of mercy for us, I trust in You!* (*Diary*, 187) (Repeat three times.) (Optional)

Our Father...

Hail Mary...

Apostles' Creed...

Decade 1. Denial by Peter

Eternal Father, I offer You the Body and Blood, Soul and Divinity of Your Dearly Beloved Son, Our Lord, Jesus Christ, in atonement for our sins and those of the whole world. (*Diary*, 476)

On each "*Hail Mary*" bead, pray: ***For the sake of His sorrowful Passion, have mercy on us and on the whole world.*** (*Diary*, 476)

1. ***For the sake...*** But Peter was following him at a distance, as far as the courtyard of the high priest; (Jn 18:58a, NRSV)

2. ***For the sake...*** While Peter was below in the courtyard, one of the servant-girls of the high priest came by. (Mk 14:66, NRSV)

3. ***For the sake...*** When she saw Peter warming himself, she stared at him and said, "You also were with Jesus, the man from Nazareth." (Mk 14:67, NRSV)

4. ***For the sake...*** But he denied it, saying, "I do not know or understand what you are talking about." And he went out into the forecourt. Then the cock crowed. (Mk 14:68, NRSV)

5. ***For the sake...*** And the servant-girl, on seeing him, began again to say to the bystanders, "This man is one of them." (Mk 14:69, NRSV)

6. ***For the sake...*** But again he denied it. Then after a little while the bystanders again said to Peter, "Certainly you are one of them; for you are a Galilean." (Mk 14:70, NRSV)

7. ***For the sake...*** One of the slaves of the high priest, a relative of the man whose ear Peter had cut off, asked, "Did I not see you in the garden with him?" (Jn 18:26, NRSV)

8. ***For the sake...*** But he began to curse, and he swore an oath, "I do not know this man you are talking about." (Mk 14:71, NRSV)

9. ***For the sake...*** At that moment the cock crowed for the second time. Then Peter remembered that Jesus had said to him, (Mk 14:72a,

NRSV)

Peter's Denial / Carl Heinrich Bloch (c. 1865-1879) / Frederiksborg Palace, Hillerød, Denmark / Wikipedia Commons {PD-old-100}

10. ***For the sake...*** "Before the cock crows twice, you will deny me three times." And he broke down and wept. (Mk 14:72b, NRSV)

Decade 2. Trial Before Sanhedrin

Eternal Father, *I offer You the Body and Blood, Soul and Divinity of Your Dearly Beloved Son, Our Lord, Jesus Christ, in atonement for our sins and those of the whole world.* (*Diary*, 476)

On each "*Hail Mary*" bead, pray: ***For the sake of His sorrowful Passion, have mercy on us and on the whole world.*** (*Diary*, 476)

1. ***For the sake...*** Those who had arrested Jesus took him to Caiaphas, the high priest, in whose house the scribes and the elders had gathered. (Mt 26:57, NRSV)

2. ***For the sake...*** Now the chief priests and the whole council were looking for false testimony against Jesus so that they might put him to death, (Mt 26:59, NRSV)

3. ***For the sake...*** but they found none, though many false witnesses came forward. At last two came forward and said, (Mt 26:60-61a, NRSV)

4. ***For the sake...*** "This fellow said, 'I am able to destroy the temple of God and to build it in three days.'" (Mt 26:61b, NRSV)

5. ***For the sake...*** The high priest stood up and said, "Have you no answer? What is it that they testify against you?" (Mt 26:62, NRSV)

6. ***For the sake...*** But Jesus was silent. Then the high priest said to him, "I put you under oath before the living God, tell us if you are the Messiah, the Son of God." (Mt 26:63, NRSV)

7. ***For the sake...*** Jesus said to him, "You have said so. But I tell you, from now on you will see the Son of Man seated at the right hand of Power and coming on the clouds of heaven." (Mt 26:64, NRSV)

8. ***For the sake...*** Then the high priest tore his clothes and said, "He has blasphemed! Why do we still need witnesses? You have now heard his blasphemy. (Mt 26:65, NRSV)

9. ***For the sake...*** What is your verdict?" They answered, "He deserves death." (Mt 26:66, NRSV)

10. ***For the sake...*** Then they spat in his face and struck him; and some slapped him, saying, "Prophesy to us, you Messiah! Who is it that struck you?" (Mt 26:67-68, NRSV)

Christ before the High Priest / Gerard van Honthorst (c. 1617) / National Gallery, London / Wikipedia Commons Public {Domain Art {PD-old-100}}

Decade 3. Pilate Sends Jesus to Herod

Eternal Father, I offer You the Body and Blood, Soul and Divinity of Your Dearly Beloved Son, Our Lord, Jesus Christ, in atonement for our sins and those of the whole world. (*Diary*, 476)

On each "*Hail Mary*" bead, pray: ***For the sake of His sorrowful Passion, have mercy on us and on the whole world.*** (*Diary*, 476)

1. ***For the sake...*** Then the assembly rose as a body and brought Jesus before Pilate. (Lk 23:1, NRSV)

2. ***For the sake...*** They began to accuse him, saying, "We found this man perverting our nation, forbidding us to pay taxes to the emperor, and saying that he himself is the Messiah, a king." (Lk 23:2, NRSV)

3. ***For the sake...*** Then Pilate said to the chief priests and the crowds, "I find no basis for an accusation against this man." (Lk 23:4, NRSV)

4. ***For the sake...*** But they were insistent and said, "He stirs up the people by teaching throughout all Judea, from Galilee where he began even to this place." (Lk 23:5, NRSV)

5. ***For the sake...*** When Pilate heard this, he asked whether the man was a Galilean. (Lk 23:6, NRSV)

6. ***For the sake...*** And when he learned that he was under Herod's jurisdiction, he sent him off to Herod, who was himself in Jerusalem at that time. (Lk 23:7, NRSV)

7. ***For the sake...*** When Herod saw Jesus, he was very glad, for he had been wanting to see him for a long time, because he had heard about him and was hoping to see him perform some sign. (Lk 23:8, NRSV)

8. ***For the sake...*** He questioned him at some length, but Jesus gave him no answer. (Lk 23:9, NRSV)

Christ Before Herod / Duccio di Buoninsegna (c. 1308-1311) / Museo dell'Opera Metropolitana del Duomo, Sienna, Italy / Wikipedia Commons {PD-old-100}

9. ***For the sake...*** The chief priests and the scribes stood by, vehemently accusing him. (Lk 23:10, NRSV)

10. ***For the sake...*** Even Herod with his soldiers treated him with contempt and mocked him; then he put an elegant robe on him, and sent him back to Pilate. (Lk 23:11, NRSV)

Decade 4. Jesus Stands Before Pilate

Eternal Father, I offer You the Body and Blood, Soul and Divinity of Your Dearly Beloved Son, Our Lord, Jesus Christ, in atonement for our sins and those of the whole world. (*Diary*, 476)

On each "*Hail Mary*" bead, pray: ***For the sake of His sorrowful Passion, have mercy on us and on the whole world.*** (*Diary*, 476)

1. ***For the sake...*** Pilate then called together the chief priests, the leaders, and the people, and said to them, "You brought me this man as one who was perverting the people; (Lk 23:13-14a, NRSV)

2. ***For the sake...*** and here I have examined him in your presence and have not found this man guilty of any of your charges against him. (Lk13:14b, NRSV)

3. ***For the sake...*** Neither has Herod, for he sent him back to us. Indeed, he has done nothing to deserve death." (Lk 23:15, NRSV)

4. ***For the sake...*** They answered, "If this man were not a criminal, we would not have handed him over to you." (Jn 18:30, NRSV)

5. ***For the sake...*** Pilate said to them, "Take him yourselves and judge him according to your law." The Jews replied, "We are not permitted to put anyone to death." (Jn 18:31, NRSV)

6. ***For the sake...*** Then Pilate entered the headquarters again, summoned Jesus, and asked him, "Are you the King of the Jews?" Jesus answered, "Do you ask this on your own, or did others tell you about me?" (Jn 18:33-34, NRSV)

7. ***For the sake...*** Pilate replied, "I am not a Jew, am I? Your own nation and the chief priests have handed you over to me. What have you done?" (Jn 18:35, NRSV)

8. ***For the sake...*** Jesus answered, "My kingdom is not from this world. If my kingdom were from this world, my followers would be fighting to keep me from being handed over to the Jews. But as it is, my kingdom is not from here." (Jn 18:36a, NRSV)

9. ***For the sake...*** Pilate asked him, "So you are a king?" Jesus answered, "You say that I am a king. For this I was born, and for this I came into the world, to testify to the truth. (Jn 18:37a, NRSV)

10. ***For the sake...*** Everyone who belongs to the truth listens to my voice." Pilate asked him, "What is truth?" (Jn 18:37b-38, NRSV)

"What is truth?" Christ before Pilate / Nikolai Ge (c. 1890) / Tretyakov Gallery, Moscow, Russia / Wikipedia Commons {PD-old-100}

Decade 5. Crucify Him

Eternal Father, I offer You the Body and Blood, Soul and Divinity of Your Dearly Beloved Son, Our Lord, Jesus Christ, in atonement for our sins and those of the whole world. (*Diary*, 476)

On each "*Hail Mary*" bead, pray: ***For the sake of His sorrowful Passion, have mercy on us and on the whole world.*** (*Diary*, 476)

1. ***For the sake...*** Now at the festival the governor was accustomed to release a prisoner for the crowd, anyone whom they wanted. (Mt 27:15, NRSV)

2. ***For the sake...*** At that time they had a notorious prisoner, called [...]Barabbas. (Mt 27:16, NRSV)

3. ***For the sake...*** So after they had gathered, Pilate said to them, "Whom do you want me to release for you, [...] Barabbas or Jesus who is called the Messiah?" (Mt 27:17, NRSV)

4. ***For the sake...*** For he realized that it was out of jealousy that they had handed him over. (Mt 27:18, NRSV)

5. ***For the sake...*** While he was sitting on the judgment seat, his wife sent word to him, "Have nothing to do with that innocent man, for today I have suffered a great deal because of a dream about him." (Mt 27:19, NRSV)

6. ***For the sake...*** Now the chief priests and the elders persuaded the crowds to ask for Barabbas and to have Jesus killed. (Mt 27:20, NRSV)

7. ***For the sake...*** The governor again said to them, "Which of the two do you want me to release for you?" And they said, "Barabbas." (Jn 18:21, NRSV)

8. ***For the sake...*** Pilate said to them, "Then what should I do with Jesus who is called the Messiah?" All of them said, "Let him be crucified!" (Mt 27:22, NRSV)

Behold the Man! / Antonio Ciseri (c. 1860-1880) / Museo d'Arte Lugano, Switzerland / Wikipedia Commons {PD-old-100}

9. ***For the sake...*** Then he asked, "Why, what evil has he done?" But they shouted all the more, "Let him be crucified!" (Jn18:23, NRSV)

10. ***For the sake...*** So when Pilate saw that he could do nothing, but rather that a riot was beginning, he took some water and washed his hands before the crowd, saying, "I am innocent of this man's blood; see to it yourselves." (Mt 27:24, NRSV)

Closing Prayers

Holy God, Holy Mighty One, Holy Immortal One, have mercy on us and on the whole world. (Repeat three times.) (*Diary*, 476)

Eternal God, *in whom mercy is endless and the treasury of compassion inexhaustible, look kindly upon us and increase Your mercy in us, that in difficult moments we might not despair nor become despondent, but with great* *confidence submit ourselves to Your holy will, which is Love and Mercy itself.* (*Diary*, 950) (Optional)

Sign of the Cross...

SEQUENCE III – SCRIPTURE & ART MEDITATIONS

- **Decade 1. The Way to Calvary** – Scourged, crowned with thorns, and mocked, Jesus makes His way to the Cross.
- **Decade 2. Jesus Is Nailed to the Cross** – Our Lord is stripped and nailed to the cross between two thieves.
- **Decade 3. Jesus Hangs on the Cross** – Christ extends mercy to the repentant thief and gives His mother to the whole world.
- **Decade 4. Jesus Dies on the Cross** – In perfect submission to the will of the Father, Jesus gives up His Spirit.
- **Decade 5. Blood and Water Gush Forth** – The living fountain of Mercy opens up for the whole world.

Introductory Prayers

Sign of the Cross...

***You expired, Jesus**, but the source of life gushed forth for souls, and the ocean of mercy opened up for the whole world. O Fount of Life, unfathomable Divine Mercy, envelop the whole world and empty Yourself out upon us.* (*Diary*, 1319) (Optional)

***O Blood and Water**, which gushed forth from the Heart of Jesus as a fount of mercy for us, I trust in You!* (*Diary*, 187) (Repeat three times.) (Optional)

Our Father...

Hail Mary...

Apostles' Creed...

Decade 1. The Way to Calvary

Eternal Father, I offer You the Body and Blood, Soul and Divinity of Your Dearly Beloved Son, Our Lord, Jesus Christ, in atonement for our sins and those of the whole world. (*Diary*, 476)

On each "*Hail Mary*" bead, pray: ***For the sake of His sorrowful Passion, have mercy on us and on the whole world.*** (*Diary*, 476)

1. ***For the sake...*** So Pilate, wishing to satisfy the crowd, released Barabbas for them; and after flogging Jesus, he handed him over to be crucified. (Mk 15:15, NRSV)

2. ***For the sake...*** Then the soldiers led him into the courtyard of the palace (that is, the governor's headquarters); and they called together the whole cohort. (Mk 15:16, NRSV)

3. ***For the sake...*** And they clothed him in a purple cloak; and after twisting some thorns into a crown, they put it on him. (Mk 15:17, NRSV)

4. ***For the sake...*** And they began saluting him, "Hail, King of the Jews!" (Mk 15:18, NRSV)

5. ***For the sake...*** They struck his head with a reed, spat upon him, and knelt down in homage to him. (Mk 15:19, NRSV)

6. ***For the sake...*** After mocking him, they stripped him of the purple cloak and put his own clothes on him. Then they led him out to crucify him. (Mk 15:20, NRSV)

7. ***For the sake...*** As they led him away, they seized a man, Simon of Cyrene, who was coming from the country, and they laid the cross on him, and made him carry it behind Jesus. (Lk 23:26, NRSV)

8. ***For the sake...*** A great number of the people followed him, and among them were women who were beating their breasts and wailing for him. (Lk 23:27, NRSV)

Christ Carrying the Cross / Titian (c. 1560) / Prado National Museum, Madrid / Wikipedia Commons {PD-old-100}

9. ***For the sake...*** But Jesus turned to them and said, "Daughters of Jerusalem, do not weep for me, but weep for yourselves and for your children. (Lk 23:28, NRSV)

10. ***For the sake...*** For the days are surely coming when they will say, 'Blessed are the barren, and the wombs that never bore, and the breasts that never nursed.'" (Lk 23:29, NRSV)

Decade 2. Jesus is Nailed to the Cross

Eternal Father, I offer you the Body and Blood, Soul and Divinity of Your Dearly Beloved Son, Our Lord, Jesus Christ, in atonement for our sins and those of the whole world. (*Diary*, 476)

On each "*Hail Mary*" bead, pray: ***For the sake of His sorrowful Passion, have mercy on us and on the whole world.*** (*Diary*, 476)

1. ***For the sake...*** When they came to the place that is called The Skull, they crucified Jesus there with the criminals, one on his right and one on his left. (Lk 23:33, NRSV)

2. ***For the sake...*** Then Jesus said, "Father, forgive them; for they do not know what they are doing." (Lk 23:34a, NRSV)

3. ***For the sake...*** It was nine o'clock in the morning when they crucified him. (Mk 15:25, NRSV)

The First Nail/ James Tissot (c. 1886-1894) / Brooklyn Museum, New York City / Wikipedia Commons {PD-old-100}

4. ***For the sake...*** [T]hey offered him wine to drink, mixed with gall; but when he tasted it, he would not drink it. (Mt 27:34, NRSV)

5. ***For the sake...*** And when they had crucified him, they divided his clothes among themselves by casting lots; (Mt 27: 35, NRSV)

6. ***For the sake...*** Pilate also had an inscription written and put on the cross. It read, "Jesus of Nazareth, the King of the Jews." (Jn 19:19, NRSV)

7. ***For the sake...*** Those who passed by derided him, shaking their heads and saying, "You who would destroy the temple and build it

in three days, save yourself! (Mt 27:39-40a, NRSV)

8. ***For the sake...*** If you are the Son of God, come down from the cross." (Mt 27:40b, NRSV)

9. ***For the sake...*** In the same way the chief priests, along with the scribes, were also mocking him among themselves and saying, "He saved others; he cannot save himself. (Mk 15:31, NRSV)

10. ***For the sake...*** Let the Messiah, the King of Israel, come down from the cross now, so that we may see and believe." (Mk 15:32, NRSV)

Decade 3. Jesus Hangs on the Cross

Eternal Father, I offer you the Body and Blood, Soul and Divinity of Your Dearly Beloved Son, Our Lord, Jesus Christ, in atonement for our sins and those of the whole world. (*Diary*, 476)

On each "*Hail Mary*" bead, pray: ***For the sake of His sorrowful Passion, have mercy on us and on the whole world.*** (*Diary*, 476)

1. ***For the sake...*** One of the criminals who were hanged there kept deriding him and saying, "Are you not the Messiah? Save yourself and us!" (Lk 23:39, NRSV)

2. ***For the sake...*** But the other rebuked him, saying, "Do you not fear God, since you are under the same sentence of condemnation? (Lk 23:40, NRSV)

3. ***For the sake...*** And we indeed have been condemned justly, for we are getting what we deserve for our deeds, but this man has done nothing wrong." (Lk 23:41, NRSV)

4. ***For the sake...*** Then he said, "Jesus, remember me when you come into your kingdom." (Lk 23:42, NRSV)

5. ***For the sake...*** He replied, "Truly I tell you, today you will be with me in Paradise." (Lk 23:43, NRSV)

Calvary / Jan Snellinck (c. 1597) / Royal Museum of Fine Arts, Antwerp, Belgium / Wikipedia Commons {PD-old-100}

6. ***For the sake...*** Meanwhile, standing near the cross of Jesus were his mother, and his mother's sister, Mary the wife of Clopas, and Mary Magdalene. (Jn 19:25b, NRSV)

7. ***For the sake...*** When Jesus saw his mother and the disciple whom he loved standing beside her, he said to his mother, "Woman, here is your son." (Jn 19:26, NRSV)

8. ***For the sake...*** Then he said to the disciple, "Here is your mother." And from that hour the disciple took her into his own home. (Jn 19:27, NRSV)

9. ***For the sake...*** When it was noon, darkness came over the whole land until three in the afternoon. (Lk 23:33, NRSV)

10. ***For the sake...*** At three o'clock Jesus cried out with a loud voice, "Eloi, Eloi, lema sabachthani?" which means, "My God, my God, why have you forsaken me?" (Lk 23:34, NRSV)

Decade 4. Jesus Dies on the Cross

Eternal Father, I offer you the Body and Blood, Soul and Divinity of Your Dearly Beloved Son, Our Lord, Jesus Christ, in atonement for our sins and those of the whole world. (*Diary*, 476)

On each "*Hail Mary*" bead, pray: ***For the sake of His sorrowful Passion, have mercy on us and on the whole world.*** (*Diary*, 476)

1. ***For the sake...*** After this, when Jesus knew that all was now finished, he said (in order to fulfill the scripture), "I am thirsty." (Jn 19:28, NRSV)

2. ***For the sake...*** When some of the bystanders heard it, they said, "This man is calling for Elijah." (Mt 27:47, NRSV)

3. ***For the sake...*** At once one of them ran and got a sponge, filled it with sour wine, put it on a stick, and gave it to him to drink. (Mt 27:48, NRSV)

4. ***For the sake...*** But the others said, "Wait, let us see whether Elijah will come to save him." (Mt 27:49, NRSV)

5. ***For the sake...*** Then Jesus, crying with a loud voice, said, "Father, into your hands I commend my spirit." (Lk 23:46a, NRSV)

Christ on the Cross / Francisco de Zurbarán (c.1627) / Art Institute of Chicago / Wikipedia Commons {PD-old-100}

6. ***For the sake...*** When Jesus had received the wine, he said, "It is finished." Then he bowed his head and gave up his spirit. (Jn 19:30,

NRSV)

7. ***For the sake...*** And the curtain of the temple was torn in two, from top to bottom. (Mk 15:38, NRSV)

8. ***For the sake...*** Now when the centurion, who stood facing him, saw that in this way he breathed his last, he said, "Truly this man was God's Son!" (Mk 15:39, NRSV)

9. ***For the sake...*** And when all the crowds who had gathered there for this spectacle saw what had taken place, they returned home, beating their breasts. (Lk 23:48, NRSV)

10. ***For the sake...*** But all his acquaintances, including the women who had followed him from Galilee, stood at a distance, watching these things. (Lk 23:49, NRSV)

Decade 5. Blood and Water Gush Forth

Eternal Father, I offer you the Body and Blood, Soul and Divinity of Your Dearly Beloved Son, Our Lord, Jesus Christ, in atonement for our sins and those of the whole world. (*Diary*, 476)

On each "*Hail Mary*" bead, pray: ***For the sake of His sorrowful Passion, have mercy on us and on the whole world.*** (*Diary*, 476)

1. ***For the sake...*** Since it was the day of Preparation, the Jews did not want the bodies left on the cross during the sabbath, especially because that sabbath was a day of great solemnity. (Jn 19:31a, NRSV)

2. ***For the sake...*** So they asked Pilate to have the legs of the crucified men broken and the bodies removed. (Jn 19:31b, NRSV)

3. ***For the sake...*** Then the soldiers came and broke the legs of the first and of the other who had been crucified with him. (Jn 19:32, NRSV)

4. ***For the sake...*** But when they came to Jesus and saw that he was already dead, they did not break his legs. (Jn 19:33, NRSV)

Peter Paul Rubens / Crucifixion (c. 1620) / Royal Museum of Fine Arts, Antwerp, Belgium / Wikipedia Commons {PD-old-100}

5. ***For the sake...*** Instead, one of the soldiers pierced his side with a spear, and at once blood and water came out. (Jn 19:34, NRSV)

6. ***For the sake...*** (He who saw this has testified so that you also may believe. His testimony is true, and he knows that he tells the

truth.) (Jn 19:35, NRSV)

7. ***For the sake...*** These things occurred so that the scripture might be fulfilled, "None of his bones shall be broken." (Jn 19:36, NRSV)

8. ***For the sake...*** And again another passage of scripture says, "They will look on the one whom they have pierced." (Jn 19:37, NRSV)

9. ***For the sake...*** Now there was a garden in the place where he was crucified, and in the garden there was a new tomb in which no one had ever been laid. (Jn 19:41, NRSV)

10. ***For the sake...*** And so, because it was the Jewish day of Preparation, and the tomb was nearby, they laid Jesus there. (Jn 19:42, NRSV)

Closing Prayers

Holy God, Holy Mighty One, Holy Immortal One, have mercy on us and on the whole world. (Repeat three times.) (*Diary*, 476)

Eternal God*, in whom mercy is endless and the treasury of compassion inexhaustible, look kindly upon us and increase Your mercy in us, that in difficult moments we might not despair nor become despondent, but with great confidence submit ourselves to Your holy will, which is Love and Mercy itself.* (*Diary*, 950) (Optional)

Sign of the Cross...

VERONICA

The Fourth of the set of Seven Stations carved by Adam Krafft at Nuremberg (c. 1490-1505) It will be noticed that the Carving is set in the wall of a house. *See p. 63.*

The inscription runs: "Hier hat Cristus sein heiligs angesicht der heiligen Frau Veronica auf iren Slayr gedruckt vor irem Haus Vc (500) Sritt von Pilatus Haws.—Here has Christ left the impress of His holy Face for the holy woman Veronica upon her veil in front of her house, 500 paces from Pilate's House."

Veronica - The fourth of the set of seven Stations of the Cross carved by Adam Krafft at Nuremberg (circa before 1490) / Source: Fr. Herbert Thurston, S.J., "The Stations of the Cross: Account of Their History and Devotional Purpose," (London: Burns and Oates, 1914), archive.org, {Public Domain {PD-old-100}}

CHAPTER 8

STATIONS OF THE CROSS & ART MEDITATIONS

As noted in her *Diary*, Jesus asked St. Faustina to honor the hour of his death—the three o'clock hour—as her duties would allow, especially by making the Stations of the Cross. Most Catholics are familiar with praying the Stations of the Cross on Fridays during Lent, and at least on Good Friday.

At this point, you may be thinking, "I try to pray the Rosary and the Divine Mercy Chaplet daily, am I to add the Stations of the Cross each day, too?"

This chapter is *not* about making the Stations of the Cross part of your daily prayer life. Instead, it is about using the Stations of the Cross as a visual meditation aid while praying the Divine Mercy Chaplet.

When I first began praying the Divine Mercy Chaplet, my work schedule allowed me to attend daily Mass. After Mass, when the Church would clear out, I'd walk around the plaques on the sidewalls using for the fourteen Stations of the Cross while praying the Divine Mercy Chaplet.

The relief plaques of the Stations of the Cross focused my meditations on Christ's passion and death while praying the Divine Mercy Chaplet. For those who pray the Divine Mercy Chaplet daily, having a visual change can be useful and stimulate new meditations.

What we call the traditional form of the Stations of the Cross has been in use since the 17th Century, formalized by Pope Clement XII in 1730, and includes those St. Faustina would have prayed during her lifetime.[1]

1. Jesus is condemned to death.
2. Jesus takes His cross.
3. Jesus falls for the first time.
4. Jesus meets His mother, Mary.
5. Simon of Cyrene helps Jesus carry the cross.
6. Veronica wipes the face of Jesus.
7. Jesus falls for the second time.
8. Jesus meets the women of Jerusalem.
9. Jesus falls for the third time.
10. Jesus is stripped of His clothes.
11. Jesus is nailed to the cross.
12. Jesus dies on the cross.
13. Jesus is taken down from the cross.
14. Jesus is placed in the tomb.

However, this exact list of fourteen stations was not always the case. A detailed history of Stations of the Cross by Fr. Herbert Thurston, S.J., documents that the stations evolved from pilgrims walking along the Via Dolorosa in the Old City of Jerusalem, as they recounted the painful journey of Christ to Calvary.[2]

Around the mid-1500s, the term "station" was first used to mark the route used and stops made by the pilgrims. The total number of "stations," including which specific sites served as stops, has changed over time.

During the last fifty years, some churches have added a fifteenth station of the cross, Resurrection of Jesus, omitted on Good Friday. The fifteenth station ends on an upbeat note, which some have attributed to the Cursillo movement.[3]

When I use the Stations of the Cross as a meditation aid while praying the Divine Mercy Chaplet, Jesus's resurrection reminds me of the love and faithfulness of God the Father, the unfathomable mercy and sacrifice of God the Son, and the guidance and the comfort of God the Holy Spirit.

The rubrics of the Catholic Church do not govern the Stations of the Cross as they are a private devotion. In this chapter, I break the Stations of the Cross up into three Sequences, similar to Chapter 7. By adding in a fifteenth station, the Resurrection, the three meditation sequences fit perfectly, each with five decades.

I have included a short sentence of reflection of mine for each bead within each decade. Using the visualization techniques of St Ignatius of Loyola, I see myself as accompanying Jesus when the events of the Stations of the Cross take place. Thus I have written my meditations as if I am present.

SEQUENCE I – STATIONS OF THE CROSS & ART MEDITATIONS

- **Decade 1. First Station:** Jesus is condemned to death.
- **Decade 2. Second Station:** Jesus takes His cross.
- **Decade 3. Third Station:** Jesus falls for the first time.
- **Decade 4. Fourth Station:** Jesus meets His mother, Mary.
- **Decade 5. Fifth Station:** Simon of Cyrene helps Jesus carry the cross.

> ***Oh, how much that*** [distrust] ***wounds My Heart! Remember My Passion, and if you do not believe My words, at least believe My wounds.*** *(Diary*, 379)

Introductory Prayers

Sign of the Cross...

You expired, Jesus, *but the source of life gushed forth for souls, and the ocean of mercy opened up for the whole world. O Fount of Life, unfathomable Divine Mercy, envelop the whole world and empty Yourself out upon us.* (*Diary*, 1319) (Optional)

O Blood and Water, *which gushed forth from the Heart of Jesus as a fount of mercy for us, I trust in You!* (*Diary*, 187) (Repeat three times.) (Optional)

Our Father...

Hail Mary...

Apostles' Creed...

Decade 1. Jesus is condemned to death

Eternal Father, I offer you the Body and Blood, Soul and Divinity of Your Dearly Beloved Son, Our Lord, Jesus Christ, in atonement for our sins and those of the whole world. (*Diary*, 476)

On each "*Hail Mary*" bead, pray:

For the sake of His sorrowful Passion, have mercy on us and on the whole world. (*Diary*, 476)

1. ***For the sake...*** O Perfect One, with no trace of sin, You stand judged and condemned to death.

2. ***For the sake...*** And who are Your judges? Those whose only power comes from God the Father.

3. ***For the sake...*** Co-eternal with the Father and the Spirit, You, the Son of God, are pronounced guilty of blasphemy.

4. ***For the sake...*** Lamb of God, You come to initiate true peace on earth and are charged with disturbing the peace.

5. ***For the sake...*** You stand silently and gaze upwards with loving submission to the will of Your Father.

6. ***For the sake...*** You told St. Faustina that we could not even know the state of our souls.

7. ***For the sake...*** Preserve us from judging the souls of others.

8. ***For the sake...*** At the hour of my death, stand as the Merciful Savior and not the Just Judge.

9. ***For the sake...*** Incline my will to that of the Father through Your Spirit.

10. ***For the sake...*** Jesus, I trust in You.

1st Station of the Cross: Jesus is condemned to death / *Basilica of the Sacred Heart of Jesus, Zagreb, Croatia* / *@ Zvonimir Atletic* / *Shutterstock.com*

Decade 2. Jesus takes His cross

Eternal Father, I offer You the Body and Blood, Soul and Divinity of Your Dearly Beloved Son, Our Lord, Jesus Christ, in atonement for our sins and those of the whole world. (*Diary*, 476)

On each "*Hail Mary*" bead, pray:

For the sake of His sorrowful Passion, have mercy on us and on the whole world. (*Diary*, 476)

1. ***For the sake...*** You accept the cross placed on Your lacerated shoulders for the love of the Father and all of humanity.

2. ***For the sake...*** The massive wooden beam rips at Your flesh already torn from the scourging—wounds that become the salve for all human pain.

3. ***For the sake...*** Innocent of any crime and with full knowledge of the suffering and torture to come, You trudge onward to Golgotha.

4. ***For the sake...*** The weight of the cross is amplified by all those who will refuse Your gifts of mercy and salvation.

5. ***For the sake...*** Forgive my periods of fear and blindness when I hid from You, thinking my sins were too big for Your Mercy.

6. ***For the sake...*** May those, yet to accept Your merciful help in shouldering their burdens in this life, be infused with trust.

7. ***For the sake...*** Unite my times of mental, physical, and spiritual sufferings to Your cross.

8. ***For the sake...*** Help me find my way by walking behind You—for without You, I am lost.

9. ***For the sake...*** My crosses become splinters when I think of all You have suffered for me.

10. ***For the sake...*** Jesus, I trust in You.

2nd Station of the Cross: Jesus takes His cross / *Basilica of the Sacred Heart of Jesus, Zagreb, Croatia / @ Zvonimir Atletic / Shutterstock.com*

Decade 3. Jesus falls for the first time

Eternal Father, I offer You the Body and Blood, Soul and Divinity of Your Dearly Beloved Son, Our Lord, Jesus Christ, in atonement for our sins and those of the whole world. (*Diary*, 476)

On each "*Hail Mary*" bead, pray:

For the sake of His sorrowful Passion, have mercy on us and on the whole world. (*Diary*, 476)

1. ***For the sake...*** You fall, Jesus, under the weight of Your cross for the first time.

2. ***For the sake...*** Hunger, thirst, weariness, blood loss, and the sins of the whole world bear down on You.

3. ***For the sake...*** Needlessly, the soldiers beat You and harshly yank You up, for nothing will stop You from carrying the cross of salvation.

4. ***For the sake...*** When I fall into sin, Your hands gently help me up, so unlike the rough handling of the soldiers.

5. ***For the sake...*** May I glorify You for the obstacles in my path; everything is a gift when I unite it to Your cross.

6. ***For the sake...*** May those who don't yet feel Your loving touch, Lord, realize that Your mercy has no limits.

7. ***For the sake...*** Use my weakness as an instrument to bring hope to those who think they are beyond Your mercy.

8. ***For the sake...*** Show me how to accompany those who have fallen under the hidden cross of loneliness and alienation.

9. ***For the sake...*** Send deliverance to those who are weighed down by the cross of unforgiveness.

10. ***For the sake...*** Jesus, I trust in You

3rd Station of the Cross: Jesus falls the first time / *Basilica of the Sacred Heart of Jesus, Zagreb, Croatia / @ Zvonimir Atletic / Shutterstock.com*

Decade 4. Jesus meets His mother, Mary

Eternal Father, I offer You the Body and Blood, Soul and Divinity of Your Dearly Beloved Son, Our Lord, Jesus Christ, in atonement for our sins and those of the whole world. (*Diary*, 476)

On each "*Hail Mary*" bead, pray:

For the sake of His sorrowful Passion, have mercy on us and on the whole world. (*Diary*, 476)

1. ***For the sake...*** Mary, Mother of Mercy, extends her arms towards You as if to take upon herself the suffering of her only beloved Son.

2. ***For the sake...*** In a bittersweet encounter, Our Sorrowful Mother searches Your eyes that wordlessly communicate, "Trust in Me."

3. ***For the sake...*** Her Immaculate Heart breaks to see the flesh of her flesh so wounded and racked with pain.

4. ***For the sake...*** A sword pierces the Blessed Mother's soul, just as Simeon predicted at Your presentation in the temple.

5. ***For the sake...*** Does Mary understand the mission of Your Incarnation—to suffer and die for the sins of the whole world?

6. ***For the sake...*** Mary trusts in the unfathomable mysteries of God as You shoulder the Cross of Salvation.

7. ***For the sake...*** Mother Mary, tutor me in pure and unshakable trust so my will conforms to that of your Son and the Father.

8. ***For the sake...*** Jesus, teach me to love as You love Your Mother Mary with flawless devotion and tenderness.

9. ***For the sake...*** Mary, take my hungry, restless heart under the protection of your Immaculate Heart and unite it to your Son's Sacred Heart.

10. ***For the sake...*** Jesus, I trust in You.

4th Station of the Cross: Jesus meets His mother, Mary / *Basilica of the Sacred Heart of Jesus, Zagreb, Croatia / @ Zvonimir Atletic / Shutterstock.com*

Decade 5. Simon of Cyrene helps Jesus carry the cross

Eternal Father, I offer You the Body and Blood, Soul and Divinity of Your Dearly Beloved Son, Our Lord, Jesus Christ, in atonement for our sins and those of the whole world. (*Diary*, 476)

On each "*Hail Mary*" bead, pray:

For the sake of His sorrowful Passion, have mercy on us and on the whole world. (*Diary*, 476)

1. ***For the sake...*** The soldiers recruit Simon of Cyrene to carry Your cross for fear that You will expire before arriving at Golgotha.

2. ***For the sake...*** Looking into Your face, does Simon sense the grace of sharing the cup of Your Passion?

3. ***For the sake...*** Did Simon's testimony of walking behind You, the Son of God, convert his sons and his wife? How could it not? [4]

4. ***For the sake...*** Every day of our lives, You allow us to participate in Your passion and death.

5. ***For the sake...*** In the mystery of redemptive suffering, You allow us to unite our sufferings to Yours, Jesus.[5]

6. ***For the sake...*** Lord help me to go the second mile when forced to go the first mile for another.[6]

7. ***For the sake...*** Teach me to endure all sufferings with the heart of Your beloved daughter, St. Faustina.

8. ***For the sake...*** Destroy my self-pride when I need to accept the help of others.

9. ***For the sake...*** Increase my charity when I need to assist others at the expense of my time, talent, or treasure.

10. ***For the sake...*** Jesus, I trust in You.

5th Station of the Cross: Simon of Cyrene helps Jesus carry the cross / *Basilica of the Sacred Heart of Jesus, Zagreb, Croatia* / *@ Zvonimir Atletic* / *Shutterstock.com*

Closing Prayers

Holy God, Holy Mighty One, Holy Immortal One, have mercy on us and on the whole world. (Repeat three times.) (*Diary*, 476)

Eternal God*, in whom mercy is endless and the treasury of compassion inexhaustible, look kindly upon us and increase Your mercy in us, that in difficult moments we might not despair nor become despondent, but with great confidence submit ourselves to Your holy will, which is Love and Mercy itself.* (*Diary*, 950) (Optional)

Sign of the Cross...

SEQUENCE II – STATIONS OF THE CROSS & ART MEDITATIONS

- **Decade 1. Sixth Station:** Veronica wipes the face of Jesus.
- **Decade 2. Seventh Station:** Jesus falls for the second time.
- **Decade 3. Eighth Station:** Jesus meets the women of Jerusalem.
- **Decade 4. Ninth Station:** Jesus falls for the third time.
- **Decade 5. Tenth Station:** Jesus is stripped of His clothes.

> ***I desire that you know more profoundly the love that burns in My Heart for souls, and you will understand this when you meditate upon My Passion.*** (*Diary*, 186)

Introductory Prayers

Sign of the Cross...

***You expired, Jesus**, but the source of life gushed forth for souls, and the ocean of mercy opened up for the whole world. O Fount of Life, unfathomable Divine Mercy, envelop the whole world and empty Yourself out upon us.* (*Diary*, 1319) (Optional)

***O Blood and Water**, which gushed forth from the Heart of Jesus as a fount of mercy for us, I trust in You!* (*Diary*, 187) (Repeat three times.) (Optional)

Our Father...

Hail Mary...

Apostles' Creed...

Decade 1. Veronica wipes the face of Jesus

Eternal Father, I offer You the Body and Blood, Soul and Divinity of Your Dearly Beloved Son, Our Lord, Jesus Christ, in atonement for our sins and those of the whole world. (*Diary*, 476)

On each "*Hail Mary*" bead, pray: ***For the sake of His sorrowful Passion, have mercy on us and on the whole world.*** (*Diary*, 476)

1. ***For the sake...*** Veronica steps forward from the crowd of onlookers to wipe the blood, sweat, and dirt from Your holy face with her veil.

2. ***For the sake...*** Without fear of reprisal from the guards, she boldly reaches out to do what she can to comfort You, Jesus, my love.

3. ***For the sake...*** The image of Your wounded face remains on her veil—now a priceless memento and holy treasure.

4. ***For the sake...*** Did she know who You were, Lord? Had news reached her of the man of miracles, Jesus of Nazareth?

5. ***For the sake...*** You are the Face of God, my Jesus. Who can fathom a divine love that takes on human flesh and suffers so?

6. ***For the sake...*** Merciful Jesus, wipe my soul clean with Your gift of forgiveness.

7. ***For the sake...*** Imprint Your Holy Image upon my soul.

8. ***For the sake...*** Wipe away my iniquity and cleanse me of my sins.[7]

9. ***For the sake...*** Replace my guilt with a clean heart.

10. ***For the sake...*** Jesus, I trust in You.

6th Station of the Cross: Veronica wipes the face of Jesus / *Basilica of the Sacred Heart of Jesus, Zagreb, Croatia* / *@ Zvonimir Atletic* / *Shutterstock.com*

Decade 2. Jesus falls for the second time

Eternal Father, I offer You the Body and Blood, Soul and Divinity of Your Dearly Beloved Son, Our Lord, Jesus Christ, in atonement for our sins and those of the whole world. (*Diary*, 476)

On each "*Hail Mary*" bead, pray: ***For the sake of His sorrowful Passion, have mercy on us and on the whole world.*** (*Diary*, 476)

1. ***For the sake...*** You collapse a second time, Jesus, and withstand another ferocious beating from the soldiers.

2. ***For the sake...*** How do You keep going, my Lord? Merely the thought of Your suffering enfeebles me.

3. ***For the sake...*** Your Incarnation removes the distance between Your pain and mine; suffering and exhaustion are Your intimate companions.

4. ***For the sake...*** I fall short of what You ask of me, but You never abandon my side.

5. ***For the sake...*** Give me the grace, Lord, to follow You as I pick up my cross after yet another failure.

6. ***For the sake...*** You accompany me, Lord, in my trials and afflictions.

7. ***For the sake...*** We cannot escape the inevitable travail of this life, but with Your grace, I can offer it back to You.

8. ***For the sake...*** You are my renewal of strength, my Merciful Jesus.

9. ***For the sake...*** I lean into You, Lord, that I may accept the realities in my life that are difficult to embrace.

10. ***For the sake...*** Jesus, I trust in You.

7th Station of the Cross: Jesus falls for the second time / *Basilica of the Sacred Heart of Jesus, Zagreb, Croatia / @ Zvonimir Atletic / Shutterstock.com*

Decade 3. Jesus meets the women of Jerusalem

Eternal Father, I offer You the Body and Blood, Soul and Divinity of Your Dearly Beloved Son, Our Lord, Jesus Christ, in atonement for our sins and those of the whole world. (*Diary*, 476)

On each "*Hail Mary*" bead, pray: ***For the sake of His sorrowful Passion, have mercy on us and on the whole world.*** (*Diary*, 476)

1. ***For the sake...*** The women of Jerusalem desire to comfort You, but You comfort them with a gaze of unconditional love.

2. ***For the sake...*** You bless them and say not to cry for You; instead, they should brace for the terrible times ahead for them.

3. ***For the sake...*** None of us will escape our portion of Your Cross, will we, My Savior?

4. ***For the sake...*** Lift my eyes to Your Divine Face of Mercy to engulf me in Your tenderness.

5. ***For the sake...*** Equip me to step out of my comfort zone with the compassion and empathy of the women of Jerusalem.

6. ***For the sake...*** When I focus inwardly, Lord Jesus, adjust priorities to minister to Your suffering body in others.

7. ***For the sake...*** Jesus, stretch out Your hands to open hearts shut tight to Your merciful outreach.

8. ***For the sake...*** Lord, join my heart to Your Heart through the undeserved gifts of my faith and your mercy.

9. ***For the sake...*** Help me to follow You wherever you lead, Lord Jesus.

10. ***For the sake...*** Jesus, I trust in You.

8th Station of the Cross: Jesus meets the women of Jerusalem / *Basilica of the Sacred Heart of Jesus, Zagreb, Croatia / @ Zvonimir Atletic / Shutterstock.com*

Decade 4. Jesus falls for the third time

Eternal Father, I offer You the Body and Blood, Soul and Divinity of Your Dearly Beloved Son, Our Lord, Jesus Christ, in atonement for our sins and those of the whole world. (*Diary*, 476)

On each "*Hail Mary*" bead, pray: ***For the sake of His sorrowful Passion, have mercy on us and on the whole world.*** (*Diary*, 476)

1. ***For the sake...*** You collapse a third time from the agony, exhaustion, and blood loss of my ransom from sin.

2. ***For the sake...*** The crowd gasps. You fall as if dead on the dusty road. Your foolish enemies think they have crushed You.

3. ***For the sake...*** But no, Your love of the Father and His love for You, embodied in the Holy Spirit, will lift you once more on invisible wings.

4. ***For the sake...*** I entrust my failures to You, Lord; let my weakness testify to Your strength.

5. ***For the sake...*** When I fall—not if—You are there for me.

6. ***For the sake...*** My Merciful Shepherd, You carry me back to the sheepfold when I fall.

7. ***For the sake...*** I repent and turn to follow You. In my brokenness and weakness, help me shoulder my trials and tribulations.

8. ***For the sake...*** Your bloodied feet smooth and level my path, I place my feet in your footprints.

9. ***For the sake...*** Help me to lift others who have fallen under the weight of their crosses.

10. ***For the sake...*** Jesus, I trust in You.

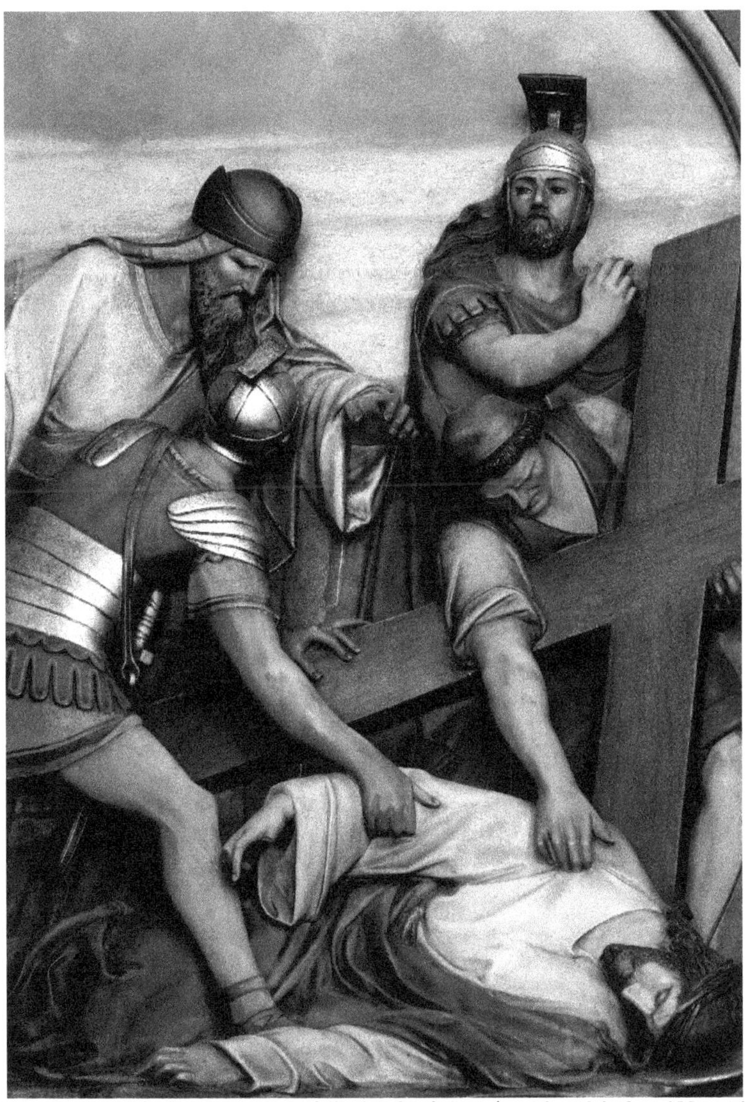

9th Station of the Cross: Jesus falls the third time / *Basilica of the Sacred Heart of Jesus, Zagreb, Croatia / @ Zvonimir Atletic / Shutterstock.com*

Decade 5. Jesus is stripped of His clothes

Eternal Father, I offer You the Body and Blood, Soul and Divinity of Your Dearly Beloved Son, Our Lord, Jesus Christ, in atonement for our sins and those of the whole world. (*Diary*, 476)

On each "*Hail Mary*" bead, pray: ***For the sake of His sorrowful Passion, have mercy on us and on the whole world.*** (*Diary*, 476)

1. ***For the sake...*** At the place of crucifixion, the soldiers roughly pull Your garments off to reveal Your nakedness.

2. ***For the sake...*** Your robe has dried into Your wounds and tear the incarnate flesh that heals our wounds of rebellion.

3. ***For the sake...*** The soldiers act to degrade You, but only debase themselves. Shame has no power over the Sinless One.

4. ***For the sake...*** You beg Father God to forgive them because they don't know Who they strip so cruelly.

5. ***For the sake...*** Lord, reveal my hidden sins that I may confess them, thereby robbing shame of power over me.

6. ***For the sake...*** Your gentleness and love towards those who torture You inspire me to overlook the slights of others.

7. ***For the sake...*** Strip me of my pride, and clothe me in the garment of Your humility.

8. ***For the sake...*** My dear Jesus, I cast off my former person to unite myself more intimately with You.

9. ***For the sake...*** May I never boast except in the humility of Your Cross.[8]

10. ***For the sake...*** Jesus, I trust in You.

10th Station of the Cross: Jesus is stripped of His clothes / *Basilica of the Sacred Heart of Jesus, Zagreb, Croatia* / *@ Zvonimir Atletic* / *Shutterstock.com*

Closing Prayers

Holy God, Holy Mighty One, Holy Immortal One, have mercy on us and on the whole world. (Repeat three times.) (*Diary*, 476)

Eternal God*, in whom mercy is endless and the treasury of compassion inexhaustible, look kindly upon us and increase Your mercy in us, that in difficult moments we might not despair nor become despondent, but with great confidence submit ourselves to Your holy will, which is Love and Mercy itself.* (*Diary*, 950) (Optional)

Sign of the Cross...

SEQUENCE III – STATIONS OF THE CROSS & ART MEDITATIONS

- **Decade 1. Eleventh Station:** Jesus is nailed to the cross.
- **Decade 2. Twelfth Station:** Jesus dies on the cross.
- **Decade 3. Thirteenth Station:** Jesus is taken down from the cross.
- **Decade 4. Fourteenth Station:** Jesus is placed in the tomb.
- **Decade 5. Fifteenth Station:** Jesus rises from the dead.

> ***I thirst. I thirst for the salvation of souls. Help Me, My daughter, to save souls. Join your sufferings to My Passion and offer them to the heavenly Father for sinners.*** (*Diary*, 1032)

Introductory Prayers

Sign of the Cross...

You expired, Jesus, *but the source of life gushed forth for souls, and the ocean of mercy opened up for the whole world. O Fount of Life, unfathomable Divine Mercy, envelop the whole world and empty Yourself out upon us.* (*Diary*, 1319) (Optional)

O Blood and Water, *which gushed forth from the Heart of Jesus as a fount of mercy for us, I trust in You!* (*Diary*, 187) (Repeat three times.) (Optional)

Our Father...

Hail Mary...

Apostles' Creed...

Decade 1. Jesus is nailed to the cross

Eternal Father, I offer You the Body and Blood, Soul and Divinity of Your Dearly Beloved Son, Our Lord, Jesus Christ, in atonement for our sins and those of the whole world. (*Diary*, 476)

On each "*Hail Mary*" bead, pray: ***For the sake of His sorrowful Passion, have mercy on us and on the whole world.*** (*Diary*, 476)

1. ***For the sake...*** The clang of the executioner's hammer echoes throughout Calvary as he drives nails into Your open, yielding hands.

2. ***For the sake...*** How do You lie so still amidst the shooting pain, my Savior?

3. ***For the sake...*** Mary reaches her hands towards You as if to take Your pain upon herself.

4. ***For the sake...*** At immense sacrifice, the marriage bed of the cross bears redemption and mercy for the whole world.

5. ***For the sake...*** Your wounds of love offer me freedom from the sins that nail my stubborn will to a cross of my own making.

6. ***For the sake...*** Not my will, but Your will be done, Lord.

7. ***For the sake...*** You know all those who will fail to trust in Your mercy—how they amplify Your suffering.

8. ***For the sake...*** Help me, Merciful Jesus, to accept Your kiss from the cross amidst sorrows, pains, hardships, and disappointments.

9. ***For the sake...*** Create poverty of spirit in me that holds all things, even my very life, in an open hand to the Father.

10. ***For the sake...*** Jesus, I trust in You.

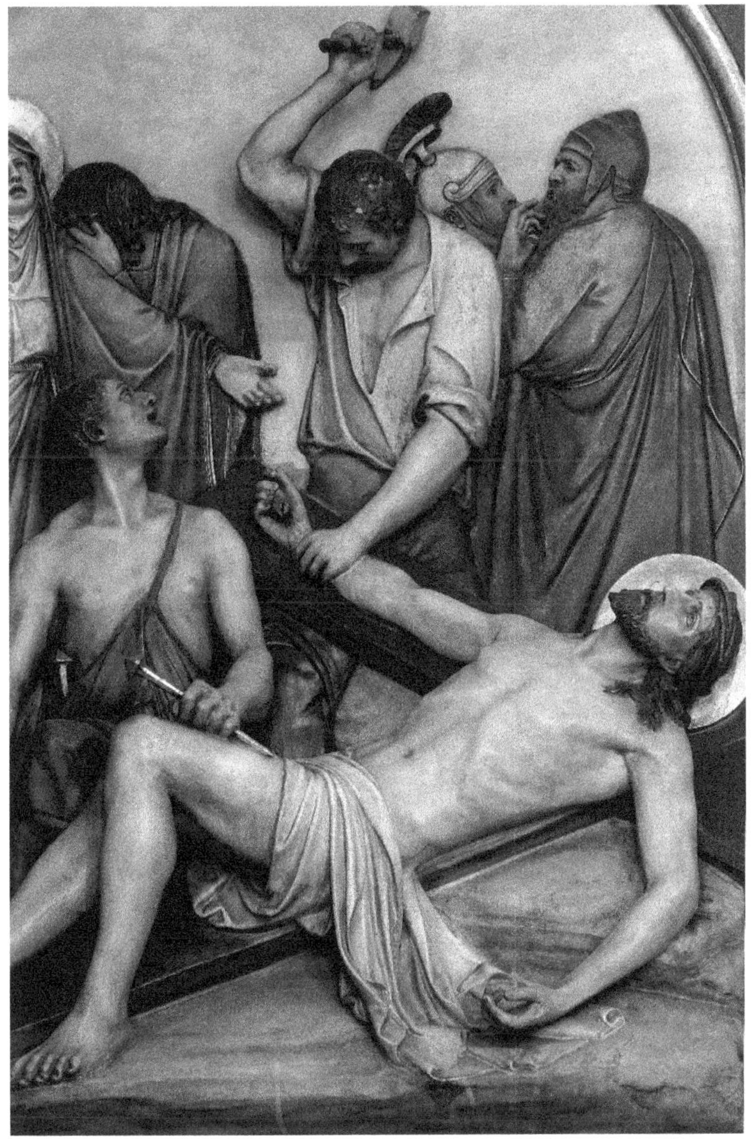

11th Station of the Cross: Jesus is nailed to the cross / *Basilica of the Sacred Heart of Jesus, Zagreb, Croatia* / *@ Zvonimir Atletic* / *Shutterstock.com*

Decade 2. Jesus dies on the cross

Eternal Father, I offer You the Body and Blood, Soul and Divinity of Your Dearly Beloved Son, Our Lord, Jesus Christ, in atonement for our sins and those of the whole world. (*Diary*, 476)

On each "*Hail Mary*" bead, pray: ***For the sake of His sorrowful Passion, have mercy on us and on the whole world.*** (*Diary*, 476)

1. ***For the sake...*** Your agony and passion end as You offer up Your Spirit to the Father; the sacrificial offering is complete.

2. ***For the sake...*** O Spotless Lamb of God, You pay my debt and that of the whole world with Your perfect sacrifice.

3. ***For the sake...*** Your Mercy gushes out in torrents of Blood and Water from Your pierced side.

4. ***For the sake...*** Help me to overcome my terror and dread of death by clinging confidently to Your Cross.

5. ***For the sake...*** May I accept my part in Your death on the Cross with humility and gratitude.

6. ***For the sake...*** You didn't escape death, nor will I. But I will not be alone; You will be with me.

7. ***For the sake...*** Displace any fear with trust, at the time of my death, resting confidently in the arms of Your Mercy.

8. ***For the sake...*** Help me to appreciate my inherent dignity and worth, made in Your Image, for which You paid an exorbitant price.

9. ***For the sake...*** Send Your comfort to the crushed and dejected who falsely believe that they are beyond Your Mercy.

10. ***For the sake...*** Jesus, I trust in You.

12th Station of the Cross: Jesus dies on the cross / *Basilica of the Sacred Heart of Jesus, Zagreb, Croatia / @ Zvonimir Atletic / Shutterstock.com*

Decade 3. Jesus is taken down from the cross

Eternal Father, I offer You the Body and Blood, Soul and Divinity of Your Dearly Beloved Son, Our Lord, Jesus Christ, in atonement for our sins and those of the whole world. (*Diary*, 476)

On each "*Hail Mary*" bead, pray: ***For the sake of His sorrowful Passion, have mercy on us and on the whole world.*** (*Diary*, 476)

1. For the sake... Mother Mary cradles Your lifeless body in her lap and lays her hand over Your stilled Sacred Heart.

2. For the sake... Mary tenderly brings Your wounded, now silent, body into her maternal embrace.

3. For the sake... With a "sword" through her heart, Mary accepts God's will, even if the final plan is unclear.

4. For the sake... Your pain was her pain, Lord Jesus, so perfectly was she united to You.

5. For the sake... You, Jesus, O Perfect Love, have willingly suffered and died for Your beloved creation.

6. For the sake... Help me to leave my self-absorption at the foot of Your Cross, Jesus, and to purify myself in your wounds.

7. For the sake... Your saving deed is the ultimate testimony of Your love for the Father and the whole world.

8. For the sake... May Mary intercede for me through her spouse, the Holy Spirit, for communion with You at the moment of my death.

9. For the sake... Mary, cradle me in your arms and carry me to Your Son's Sacred Heart when I pass from this life to the next.

10. For the sake... Jesus, I trust in You.

13th Station of the Cross: Jesus is taken down from the cross / *Basilica of the Sacred Heart of Jesus, Zagreb, Croatia / @ Zvonimir Atletic / Shutterstock.com*

Decade 4. Jesus is placed in the tomb

Eternal Father, I offer You the Body and Blood, Soul and Divinity of Your Dearly Beloved Son, Our Lord, Jesus Christ, in atonement for our sins and those of the whole world. (*Diary*, 476)

On each "*Hail Mary*" bead, pray: ***For the sake of His sorrowful Passion, have mercy on us and on the whole world.*** (*Diary*, 476)

1. ***For the sake...*** Those who are with You to the end gently wrap Your lifeless body in white linen and place Your shrouded body in the tomb.

2. ***For the sake...*** You enter into the horror and desolation of human death and, thereby, transform both.

3. ***For the sake...*** Just as my soul will leave my body at death, Your soul leaves the cold, dark tomb.

4. ***For the sake...*** You announce the Good News to those held captive previously by death, now set free by Your sacrificial death.

5. ***For the sake...*** We have only to accept your salvation, wash in Your Mercy, and repent of our transgressions.

6. ***For the sake...*** Jesus, Your Mercy is the cure for the mortality that my nature abhors.

7. ***For the sake...*** Divine Justice, satiated by Your passion and death, becomes the Divine Mercy to heal my misery and that of the whole world.

8. ***For the sake...*** King of Mercy, help me to live each day as my last.

9. ***For the sake...*** I was dead in my transgressions until You revealed the glorious Face of Your Mercy and Love to me.

10. ***For the sake...*** Jesus, I trust in You.

14th Station of the Cross: Jesus is placed in the tomb / *Basilica of the Sacred Heart of Jesus, Zagreb, Croatia / Zvonimir Atletic / Shutterstock.com*

Decade 5. Jesus rises from the dead

Eternal Father, I offer You the Body and Blood, Soul and Divinity of Your Dearly Beloved Son, Our Lord, Jesus Christ, in atonement for our sins and those of the whole world. (*Diary*, 476)

On each "*Hail Mary*" bead, pray: ***For the sake of His sorrowful Passion, have mercy on us and on the whole world.*** (*Diary*, 476)

1. ***For the sake...*** My redemption sets sail on the wings of the cross and soars to the heavens in Your resurrection.

2. ***For the sake...*** In Your resurrection, the suffering and sorrows of my life become sources of my holiness and joy.

3. ***For the sake...*** In Your glorified wounds, my deepest hopes and desires materialize.

4. ***For the sake...*** Suffering and death don't have the last word, as the glory and power of the Trinity bursts forth in Your glorified body!

5. ***For the sake...*** Your glorified body divinizes our shared humanity in the second person of the Trinity.

6. ***For the sake...*** Through Your death and resurrection, You invite me into the communion of the Trinity.

7. ***For the sake...*** Through Your resurrection, I have unfailing hope. Death is not the victor.

8. ***For the sake...*** May it no longer be me, but You, my Jesus, who lives in me.

9. ***For the sake...*** By Your death and resurrection, You fling open the floodgates of Divine Mercy.

10. ***For the sake...*** Jesus, I trust in You.

15th Station of the Cross: Jesus rises from the dead / *The Resurrection: Mosaic from a side chapel of the Rosary Basilica, Sanctuary of Our Lady of Lourdes / Lourdes, France / Preacherdoc - CC BY-SA (creativecommons.org / licenses / by-sa / 4.0)*

Closing Prayers

Holy God, Holy Mighty One, Holy Immortal One, have mercy on us and on the whole world. (Repeat three times.) (*Diary*, 476)

Eternal God, *in whom mercy is endless and the treasury of compassion inexhaustible, look kindly upon us and increase Your mercy in us, that in difficult moments we might not despair nor become despondent, but with great confidence submit ourselves to Your holy will, which is Love and Mercy itself.* (*Diary*, 950) (Optional)

Sign of the Cross...

CHAPTER 9

COMBINING THE CHAPLET WITH THE ROSARY

Someone once asked me if the Divine Mercy Chaplet was more powerful than the Rosary. I answered that they are different devotions, so it's like comparing apples to oranges. Some people prefer one to the other, but that does not make one inherently better than the other.

The Rosary is Mary's praise song to God for the work of salvation—through the promise of the Father, the sacrifice of the Son, under the guidance of the Holy Spirit (her spouse).[1] Through the Rosary, Mary directs us to her beloved Son as she always does.

In the Divine Mercy Chaplet, Jesus asks us to meditate on His passion and death while imploring the Father for mercy for each of us and the whole world.

Mary, through the Rosary, leads us to her Son, and Jesus, through the Divine Mercy Chaplet, leads us to His Father.

I pray the Rosary and the Divine Mercy Chaplet daily, not because I have heaps of time—I don't. The Rosary and Divine Mercy Chaplet are unique prayers. Mary has asked us to pray the Rosary each day, and Jesus has asked us, through St. Faustina, to pray the Divine Mercy Chaplet without ceasing. Prayer is the wellspring from which everything else in my day flows. Without prayer, I am a mess.

In the Divine Mercy Chaplet, we plead for the Father's Mercy through the holy wounds of God the Son.

The Son's passion and death signify Christ's perfect love for and obedience to the will of the Father; there is nothing more pleasing that we can offer to the Father. When God's love meets the repentant sinner, that sinner is washed clean through His mercy, thanks to Christ's restoration of our relationship with God.

There have been times in my life when I have struggled to forgive myself, which is why I latched onto the Divine Mercy Chaplet immediately after reading the *Diary* of St. Faustina in the spring of 2012, and I've never let go. I work on trusting Jesus daily as I pray the Divine Mercy Chaplet.

In 2013, I consecrated myself to the Sacred Heart of Jesus through the Immaculate Heart of Mary[2]—that was even before I was back in the full graces of the Catholic Church. Since then, everything I pray, do, have, and am, I give to Mary to purify through her Immaculate Heart and then pass onto her Son. Consequently, I visualize the prayers of my Rosary held in Mary's gentle hands and lifted to her Son.

In 1917, Our Lady of Fatima taught the three shepherd children a new prayer to conclude each decade of the Rosary,

> *O my Jesus, forgive us our sins, save us from the fires of Hell, lead all souls to Heaven, especially those in most need of Thy mercy.*[3]

The Fatima prayer links the Rosary and the Divine Mercy Chaplet with the words "*especially those in most need of Thy* **mercy** (emphasis added)." Less than ten years before Jesus taught the Divine Mercy Chaplet to St. Faustina, Mary seemed to be preparing the world for the message of Divine Mercy through her appearance to the three shepherd children.

Mary has asked us to invoke the mercy of God at the end of each decade. I consider this an invitation to unite the two devotions on the days when I meditate on the Sorrowful Mysteries.[4]

The decades of the Rosary contain five *Our Fathers*, fifty *Hail Marys*, and five *Glory Bes*. The decades of the Divine Mercy Chaplet include five *Eternal Fathers* and fifty *For the Sake of His Sorrowful Passions*.

Note that each decade of the Rosary and Divine Mercy Chaplet begins with a prayer to our Heavenly Father: the *Our Father* and the *Eternal Father*, respectively. For me, this determines the correspondence between the Rosary and the Divine Mercy Chaplet.

That and my personal decision to pray my Chaplet of Divine Mercy inside my Rosary—or equivalently through Mary's hands.

Thus, after each *Our Father* that begins a decade of the Rosary, I immediately pray the *Eternal Father* of the Divine Mercy Chaplet. After each Hail Mary within a decade, I recite the *For the Sake of His Sorrowful Passion* of the Divine Mercy Chaplet. Each decade finally concludes with the *Glory Be* and the *Fatima Prayer.*

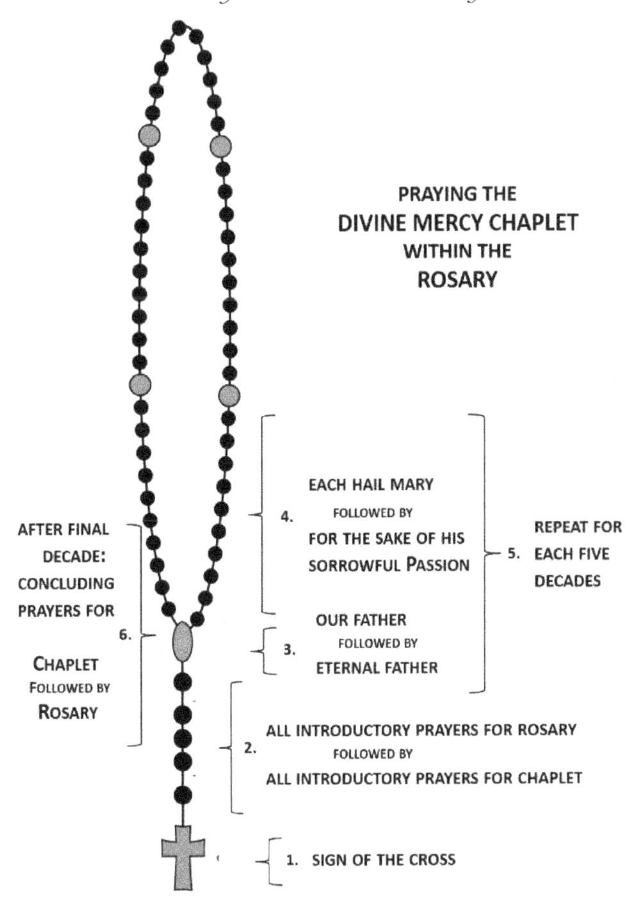

© *Thoom / Shutterstock.com / modified by MKDaly*

I lead off with the introductory prayers for my Rosary (*Sign of the Cross, Apostles' Creed, Our Father*, three *Hail Marys*, and the *Glory Be*). Next, I pray the introductory prayers for the Chaplet (*You Expired Jesus, O Blood and Water* - three times, the *Our Father*, the *Hail Mary*, and the *Apostles' Creed*).

After the fifth decade, I pray the concluding prayers for the Divine Mercy Chaplet (*Holy God* - three times and *Eternal God*). These are followed by concluding prayers of the Rosary: *Hail, Holy Queen,* and one of several final prayers. I happen to use the concluding prayers according to the Method of St. Louis de Montfort.

I use my book, *Bead by Bead: The Scriptural Rosary*, when I pray the Divine Mercy Chaplet inside my Rosary. *Bead by Bead* contains different scriptural verses and sacred art images than those found in Chapter 7 of this book.

Does one have to combine the Rosary and the Divine Mercy Chaplet this way? Of course not! Do what works for you.

Daily prayer is a habit that is formed through self-discipline and can only be acquired permanently because of one's faith in the power of prayer. When we ask for things consistent with God's will, prayer does move mountains, and even more difficult—prayer opens closed hearts! I know it opened mine.

ENDNOTES

1 - INTRODUCTION

[1] Article: thedivinemercy.org/articles/toward-new-doctor-church-saint-maria-faustina-kowalska-0, accessed online May 26, 2020.
[2] Maria Tarnawaska, *Sister Faustina—Her Life and Mission*, trans. Anne Hargest-Gorzelak, (Veritas Foundation Publication Centre, 1990), distributed by Marian Helpers, Stockbridge MA.
[3] Ewa K. Czaczkowska, *Faustina: The Mystic & Her Message*, trans. Orest Pawlak, et al., (Stockbridge MA: Marian Press, 2015).
[4] Fr. Donald Calloway, M.I.C, *Purest of Lilies*, (Stockbridge MA: Marian Press, 2015).
[5] Meggie K. Daly, *Bead by Bead: The Scriptural Rosary*, (Nashville TN: Misericordia Publishing, 2017).
[6] Ibid., pgs. 35-37. The first person I heard use the term, "God-event," was Michael E. Gaitley, MIC.

2 - DIVINE MERCY AND ME

[1] For a short explanation of the Catholic Church's annulment (declaration of nullity) process, see usccb.org/issues-and-action/marriage-and-family/marriage/annulment/index.cfm, accessed May 28, 2020.
[2] Saint Maria Faustina Kowalska, *Divine Mercy in My Soul*, (Stockbridge MA: Marian Press, 2011), para 1798.
[3] Saint Maria Faustina Kowalska, *Divine Mercy in My Soul*, para 1486.

3 - THE GREATER THE SINNER

[1] Fr. Donald Haggerty, *Conversion: Spiritual Insights into an Essential Encounter with God*, (San Francisco: Ignatius Press, 2017) See Chapter 4, The Mercy of God.

[2] The Paschal Sacrifice is the passion and death of Jesus Christ. The Paschal Mystery is the passion, death, resurrection, and ascension into heaven of Jesus Christ.
[3] Examples include but are not limited to these well-known saints: St. Catherine of Siena, St. John of the Cross, St. Saint Therese of Lisieux, St. Faustina, and St. John Paul II.
[4] For a biblical context of redemptive suffering, see Col 1:24. In redemptive suffering, we join our suffering to that of Christ's Paschal Sacrifice. It is a gift that God allows us to participate so.
[5] Saint Augustine, trans. Henry Chadwick, *Confessions*, (New York: Oxford University Press, 2008), pg. 3. Capitalization added in the text of my quote for "Yourself" and "You."
[6] Concepción Cabrera de Armida (Conchita), *What Jesus Is Like*, trans. Most Rev. Donald W. Montrose, (Staten Island, NY: Society of St. Paul/Alba House, 2019), pg.4.
[7] Ibid, pg. 7.
[8] Saint Maria Faustina Kowalska, *Divine Mercy in My Soul*, para 267.
[9] Encyclical of his Holiness John Paul II, *Dives in Misericordia*, sec. 7, from the online Vatican repository of encyclicals: www.vatican.va/content/john-paul-ii/en/encyclicals/documents/hf_jp-ii_enc_301 11980_dives-in-misericordia.html, accessed on May 26, 2020.

4 - ST. FAUSTINA'S ROLE

[1] Maria Tarnawaska, *Sister Faustina—Her Life and Mission.*
[2] Ewa K. Czaczkowska, *Faustina: The Mystic & Her Message.*
[3] Saint Maria Faustina Kowalska, *Divine Mercy in My Soul*, para 9.
[4] Ibid, para 10.
[5] This table is derived from the compilation of data from various sources, including the *Diary*, Tarnawaska, and Czaczkowska, and www.sisterfaustina.org/content/st-faustina-diary. Data are rounded.
[6] Saint Maria Faustina Kowalska, *Divine Mercy in My Soul*, para 311.
[7] Table 2 percentages are calculated based on simple page counts; months are rounded to the nearest integer.
[8] Table 3 is extracted from Donald Calloway, MIC., *Purest of all lilies: the Virgin Mary in the spirituality of St. Maria Faustina Kowalska.* Graduate Theses and Dissertations. The University of Dayton, https://ecommons.udayton.edu/graduate_theses/6594/ Click link to full text, pg. 47 in the downloaded pdf—or equivalently internal pg. 39. This thesis contains more detail than Fr. Calloway's book with the same title.

[9] Ibid, I added the first column only.
[10] Saint Maria Faustina Kowalska, *Divine Mercy in My Soul*, para 1732.
[11] Michael E. Gaitley, MIC., *The Second Greatest Story Ever Told*, (Stockbridge MA: Marian Press, 2011), p. 60. Although not in her *Diary*, St. Faustina is said to have predicted the exact day when the Germans invaded Poland during World War II.
[12] Ibid, pp. 65-70. This is a fantastic story; I am skimming the details.
[13] Canonization homily for St. Faustina: vatican.va/content/john-paul-ii/en/homilies/2000/documents/hf_jp-ii_hom_20000430_faustina.html, sections 6 and 7, accessed online May 26, 2020.
[14] Ibid, section 4.
[15] "A victim soul is an individual who has been chosen by God to undergo physical, and sometimes spiritual, suffering beyond that of normal human experience. The victim soul willingly accepts this unique and difficult mission of offering up his or her pains for the salvation of others." simplycatholic.com/what-is-a-victim-soul/, accessed online May 26, 2020.

5 - DIVINE MERCY DEVOTIONS

[1] Bishop Robert Barron, Daily Mass Word on Fire, homily: 4/26/20. youtube.com/watch?v=k9IMsuQ2CRo&feature=youtu.be&t=118 1, accessed May 26, 2020.
[2] Saint Maria Faustina Kowalska, *Divine Mercy in My Soul*, para 299.
[3] See www.marian.org/house/copyright.php for information.
[4] Canonization homily for St. Faustina: vatican.va/content/john-paul-ii/en/homilies/2000/documents/hf_jp-ii_hom_20000430_faustina.html, see section 4, accessed online May 26, 2020.
[5] Saint Maria Faustina Kowalska, *Divine Mercy in My Soul*, paras 300, 699, and 1109.
[6] One example is from the writings of Rev. Rozycki, the theologian who examined the *Diary* for the Holy See.
[7] Plenary Indulgence: ewtn.com/catholicism/devotions/conditions-13362, accessed online May 26, 2020.
[8] See article: thedivinemercy.org/articles/vatican-grants-emergency-plenary-indulgence-divine-mercy-chaplet.
[9] Two sources: 1) Saint Maria Faustina Kowalska, *Divine Mercy in My Soul*, pg. xxii 2) thedivinemercy.org/celebrate/greatgrace/graces.
[10] Saint Maria Faustina Kowalska, *Divine Mercy in My Soul*, para 754 and para 811.
[11] Ibid, para 687.

[12] Ibid, para 1541.
[13] See Mt (27:45), Mk (15:33), and Lk (23:44).
[14] Saint Maria Faustina Kowalska, *Divine Mercy in My Soul*, para 1572.
[15] DVD, "In the Name of Miracles," the story of Maureen Digan that led to the beautification of St. Faustina. shopmercy.org/in-the-name-of-miracles.html.
[16] Fr. Ron Pytel cure: baltimoresun.com/news/bs-xpm-2003-11-06-0311060226-story.html.

6 - LOGISTICS OF THE DIVINE MERCY CHAPLET

[1] Saint Maria Faustina Kowalska, *Divine Mercy in My Soul*, para 1542.
[2] Ibid, para 476.

7 - SCRIPTURE & ART MEDITATIONS

[1] usccb.org/prayer-and-worship/prayers-and-devotions/stations-of-the-cross/scriptural-stations-of-the-cross.cfm, accessed online May 26, 2020.

8 - STATIONS OF THE CROSS & ART MEDITATIONS

[1] Fr. Herbert Thurston, S.J., *The Stations of the Cross: Account of Their History and Devotional Purpose*, (London: Burns and Oates, reprinted 1914). archive.org/details/stationsofcrossa00thuruoft, accessed on May 7, 2020.
[2] Ibid. In addition, udayton.edu/imri/mary/w/way-of-the-cross-history.php, accessed on May 7, 2020.
[3] blog.franciscanmedia.org/sam/15th-station-of-the-cross, accessed on May 7, 2020.
[4] Suggested by Mk 15:21 and Rm 16:13.
[5] Suggested by Col 1:24.
[6] Suggested by Mt 5:38.
[7] See Ps 51:2.
[8] Suggested by Gal 6:14.

9 - COMBINING THE CHAPLET WITH THE ROSARY

[1] "United to the Holy Spirit as his *spouse*, she is one with God in an incomparably more perfect way than can be predicated of any other creature." – St. Maximillian Kolbe, Feb 17, 1941.
piercedhearts.org/hearts_jesus_mary/heart_mary/max_kolbe_im

maculate_conception.htm, accessed online May 26, 2020.
[2] I used the Marian Consecration format of *33 Days to Morning Glory* by Michael E. Gaitley, MIC., allheartsafire.org/33-days-to-morning-glory/overview.html, accessed online May 26, 2020.
[3] Dom Augustine Marie, OSB, *The Message of Our Lady of Fatima*, archive.org/stream/TheMessageOfOurLadyOfFatimaWithPicture/fatimaSelectionspic_djvu.txt, accessed online May 28, 2020.
[4] St. John Paul II suggested praying the Sorrowful Mysteries of the Rosary on Tuesdays and Fridays. During Lent, he suggested replacing the Glorious Mysteries with the Sorrowful Mysteries.

ABOUT THE AUTHOR

Meggie K. Daly relocated to the beautiful Pacific Northwest to be closer to her six adult children and her newest brood of grandchildren. A retired research scientist and Mathematics instructor, Meggie spent half of her life running from God or searching for a reason to believe in the Christian God. Eventually, she was given the gift of faith and wooed by the unconditional love of Jesus Christ, her Lord, and Savior. She writes when she can between providing childcare for several grandkids, facilitating classes on the spiritual life at her local Catholic parish, gardening (weeding, mostly), and eating cinnamon rolls and chocolate whenever possible. This work is her second non-fiction book.

CPSIA information can be obtained
at www.ICGtesting.com
Printed in the USA
BVHW052019160820
586495BV00004B/27

9 781735 238807